Personalized Reading

Personalized Reading

It's a Piece of PIE

Nancy Hobbs, Kristen Sacco,
and Myra R. Oleynik

LIBRARIES UNLIMITED

AN IMPRINT OF ABC-CLIO, LLC
Santa Barbara, California • Denver, Colorado • Oxford, England

Library of Congress Cataloging-in-Publication Data

Hobbs, Nancy.
   Personalized reading : it's a piece of PIE / Nancy Hobbs, Kristen Sacco, and Myra R. Oleynik.
      p. cm.
   Includes bibliographical references and index.
   ISBN 978–1–59884–522–8 (hard copy : alk. paper) — ISBN 978–1–59884–523–5 (ebook)
1. Silent reading. 2. Individualized reading instruction. 3. Children—Books and reading. I. Sacco,
Kristen. II. Oleynik, Myra R. III. Title.
   LB1050.55.H63   2011
   372.45′4—dc22   2010034864

ISBN: 978–1–59884–522–8
EISBN: 978–1–59884–523–5

15 14 13 12 11   1 2 3 4 5

This book is also available on the World Wide Web as an eBook.
Visit www.abc-clio.com for details.

Libraries Unlimited
An Imprint of ABC-CLIO, LLC

ABC-CLIO, LLC
130 Cremona Drive, P.O. Box 1911
Santa Barbara, California 93116-1911

This book is printed on acid-free paper ∞

Manufactured in the United States of America

Contents

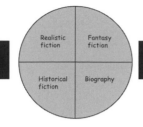

Chapter 1

Introducing PIE and How It Came to Be

Experienced educators often reach a point in their careers when they begin to examine their daily practices and analyze the value of each of the activities planned for their students. That moment came for us eight years ago. Each year, we searched for strategies that not only built the necessary reading skills for our students but also for ways to help them develop a love of reading. The later goal was a much more difficult one to achieve.

Upon examining a typical student's schedule in our elementary classroom, there was an alarming lack of time devoted to actual reading during the day. Students read a story from the basal reading series, perhaps several times during the week, and read the workbook pages that accompany the story. Students completed graphic organizers and sometimes created reading projects to help facilitate better understanding of the story, but the actual time in minutes per week that students read was traditionally very low. In most elementary classrooms across the country, the curricular skills of reading are taught every day, yet students spend very little time choosing books they would like to read, talking about the books they have read, and actually reading in the classroom.

As many teachers have done before, we turned to the commercial programs that offered incentives to students through points and prizes for reading a specified number of pages or books. Although initially these programs did seem to motivate students to achieve, they did very little to build a love of reading. We knew that students needed to develop the reading habit by reading every day, but we still had many unanswered questions:

- How can we teach our students to make good book choices?

- What strategies can we use to help our students develop a love of different genres?

- Is there someone else besides the classroom teacher who could support our students' reading goals?

- Should students have the opportunity to talk to others about the books they are reading?

- How do we make the best use of our school library in helping our students to become better readers?

- Is it a good use of the school day for students to spend time reading the books they have self-selected?

Through our creation of PIE, the *P*ersonalized, *I*ndependent *E*nrichment program, we found the answers to many of these questions.

This idea of self-selection was important so students could make personal connections with books of their choice. Although we thought it was important for students to choose their own books, we also wanted to encourage them to read books from different genres. From our classroom observations, we found that young students rarely chose books outside of the genre with which they were most familiar. It was exciting to see students take pleasure in reading a genre they had never experienced before. They also enjoyed the opportunity to talk about these books with their classmates. It was through these deep discussions that students had the chance to share their opinions and formulate real connections to the story. After these sessions, it was always fun and interesting to see students race to the library to check out the book titles that their classmates had read and shared with them.

Because book selection was such a key component of the PIE program, it made sense that both the classroom teacher and school librarian would play parts in helping students become better readers. The school librarian was the authority on the book collection and was most suited to help the students become familiar with the library. The classroom teacher knew her students' strengths and needs as developing readers. Together, these two professionals could work collaboratively to build the love of reading in all students. The power of this collaboration could span the spectrum from talking to each other as they pass in the library to eventually building a positive coalition complete with planning lessons together. This idea of collaboration is well supported by the American Association of School Librarians Reading 4 Life (AASL R4L) position statement regarding the importance of librarians and teachers partnering to achieve reading goals (Moreillon, 2007). In the PIE program, the teacher and the librarian are equal partners who share a common goal, which is helping students to become readers. This partnership distinguishes PIE from other reading incentive programs. This powerful collaboration contributes in many ways to students' reading success:

- The teacher and librarian co-teach a variety of lessons throughout the school year relating to all aspects of the reading process (e.g., characterization, setting, plot, main idea, sequencing events, making inferences).

- The teacher and librarian have frequent discussions about the kinds of books that a struggling reader might enjoy. This discussion ensures that either the teacher or the librarian will be available to that child to provide support when it is time to choose a book.

- The teacher and librarian plan Book Chats together to introduce and promote different genres.

- The teacher and librarian are both excited when students find the perfect series or the book that ignites the love of reading.

- The collaboration between the teacher and librarian becomes a positive model for sharing ideas that extends to the students as they become partners with each other.

- The familiarity with the library extends to the classroom teacher as well as the students. When the teacher views the library as an extended classroom, he or she can then facilitate discussions and activities in the library alone, if necessary.

After the books have been selected and read, we found that it was important to have a forum for students to gather and share their story with others. We compare this to the desire adults have to tell someone about a great book they recently read. The sharing of the book deepens the understanding of the story and enhances the connection of the text to the reader. In PIE, this activity occurs during the Book Sharing sessions. Students gather in small groups with the teacher, librarian, or both and retell the story through a story element summary (SES). This is an informal meeting with group members asking questions, sharing personal opinions, and commenting on similar books they have read. The conversations are spontaneous, lively, and informative. It is the kind of session that makes people walking down the hall want to stop in and listen for a while (Figure 1.1).

Our students look forward to our PIE meeting day and prepare for it throughout the week. Reading and writing about their PIE book are activities that our students are engaged in every day in the classroom. Reading silently is not just for free time; rather, it is part of our daily procedure.

Reading around the PIE truly built our love of reading in our classroom and improved the overall reading skills of our students. To get started, teachers and librarians need to form a partnership by making a commitment to work together to help students become better readers and begin to allow the magic of personalized reading through PIE to take place!

Reference

Moreillon, J. *Collaborative Strategies for Teaching Reading Comprehension: Maximizing Your Impact*. ALA Edition, 2007.

Realistic fiction

Fantasy fiction

Historical fiction

Biography

Name _____

Figure 1.1 First Four Piece PIE. Depending upon the grade level, students may begin with a 2, 3, or 4 piece PIE.

Chapter 2

Explaining the PIE Program

PIE is a Personalized, Independent Enrichment program for readers of all abilities. Students choose books from eight different genres displayed on a PIE chart. The genres include realistic fiction, fantasy, biography, historical fiction, adventure/mystery, science fiction, poetry, and nonfiction. The teacher and librarian introduce the individual genres through classroom lessons, read-alouds, and book chats.

The book selection and order of the genres read is each student's choice, making the program personal. For each book read, students are asked to maintain a reading log to track their progress. After students have finished a book, they complete a story element summary (SES). These summaries provide a framework that highlights the characters, setting, and plot of the story. Students meet in small groups with the teacher, librarian, or both on a weekly basis to share either their SES or the progress they have made on their books. After students share their SES, they write the title of the book and color that slice of the genre on their PIE chart. When all parts of the PIE are completed, the students should choose one of the books they have read and complete a project to extend their learning about that story. After students share their project with their PIE group, the process begins again with the selection of a new book based on a genre from the next PIE chart.

The program is independent because the students move through PIE charts at their own pace. Students begin the year with a four-genre PIE chart that includes realistic fiction, fantasy, biography, and historical fiction. After students have completed all of the steps for each book read, they are given a second PIE chart with four additional genres: science fiction, poetry, adventure/ mystery, and nonfiction. After this PIE chart is complete, an eight-piece PIE chart that includes all of the genres is given to the student. Students can complete as many eight-piece PIE charts as possible throughout the school year. When students have the opportunity to choose their own books, write about them, and talk about the stories with their classmates, they come to realize how books can enrich their lives (Figure 2.1).

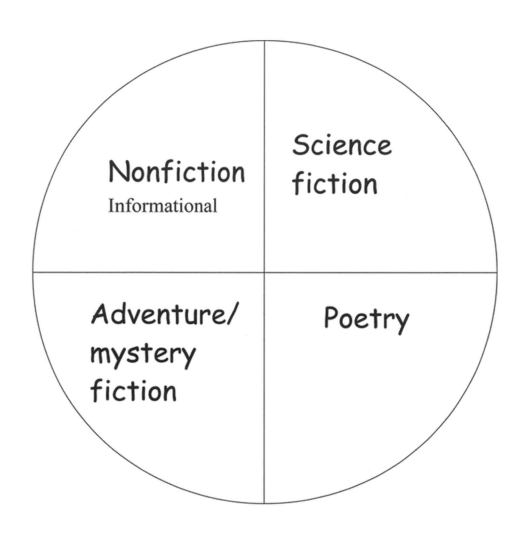

Name _____

Figure 2.1 Second Four Piece PIE. Any way you slice it, be sure to introduce new genres each time you are ready to serve a new PIE.

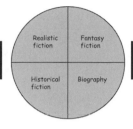

Chapter 3

Selecting the Book: The Importance of Choice

Students who actively participate in the selection of their own reading material grow into adults who read widely and take a proactive role in their own learning. In fact, the new American Association of School Librarians (AASL) Standards advise school librarians to emphasize the need for reading as a beginning skill in students' ability to learn, grow, and enjoy (AASL Standards, 2007). Most school librarians and teachers agree with this wholeheartedly, and your book authors believe that it is time to serve our hungry readers the delicious treat of personalized reading by putting it back onto the literacy menu.

The PIE (Personalized, Independent, Enrichment) program addresses these basic components by empowering young readers to open their own windows to seek the wide world of literature that awaits. And as a result, their guided efforts will naturally lead even our youngest 21st century learners on the path to personal growth and information literacy.

PIE leads our students on this journey with confidence and supports the belief from the AASL that states: "The student who is an independent learner is information literate and pursues information related to personal interests" (AASL, 1998). When given direction, frequent opportunities, and ample time, students can learn to pursue their personal interests and be taught how to select books at their appropriate reading level while also

Decisions. Decisions. Which slice of PIE should I read next?

recognizing when to abandon a book of low interest. That is one of the most important signs of independent learning on this literacy trail.

With PIE, young readers are encouraged to choose and read books at their own pace with the understanding that the goal is not to be the first one to pick a book or to read as many books as possible but to self-select an appropriate book to read for pure enjoyment and information. Students and teachers quickly come to realize that the intrinsic reward—the sweet love of reading—far outweighs any extrinsic reward such as points or prizes.

The AASL's new standards describe 21st century learners as students who demonstrate their appreciation for literature not only by choosing books to read for pleasure but also by being interested in many different literary genres. Encouraging students to read books from a variety of genres is a significant ingredient in PIE. To achieve that end, the users of the PIE program must recognize the value in allowing students to take their time in selecting their own books with a more thoughtful and deliberate approach.

Many educators simply expect this thoughtful and deliberate behavior from students without giving clear expectations, proper definitions, or strategies. As a result, too many elementary students select a book without much thought or planning. Their choice may have been a book they noticed with a friend, one with an unusual cover, or perhaps it was the closest book within reach when the bell rang. Although most students using their school library have access to a variety of books, they often have very limited understanding of how to select one, which results in students making random choices before their time runs out.

Taking the time to read the teaser.

Be sure to meet and greet every book. Two fingers down? This book is definitely OK!

Genre shelf labels and spine labels help to mark an entire shelf with its most prominent genre.

When students have had a lack of exposure to the wide range of titles, authors, and genres available, they are left feeling perplexed and often more than a little frustrated. Much research supports the benefits of self-selected reading when students are provided with guidance; tools; and most importantly, the ample time to do so. The PIE program provides all three of these elements because the teacher, librarian, and student work together as a team.

Implementing the PIE program acknowledges that choosing a book is a process. Self-selection takes practice, and students must be allowed to progress at their own pace. As a result, PIE offers a more structured recipe for success because the goal is to take students far beyond Benjamin Bloom's basic knowledge level of learning (Bloom, 1956). Success in PIE is not measured by how many books are tallied onto a chart but rather by the variety of appropriate choices made. It is a process by which students pace themselves and actually savor the selection experience. Just as we sample new foods to acquire a desired taste, such is the procedure for PIE. It recognizes the value of self-selection and promotes it through the choices of various literary genres while also encouraging students to grow with their literature on many different planes.

Through PIE, students develop as readers as they experience learning at every level of Bloom's taxonomy. And it is specifically through the act of self-selection that this wide range of student behaviors is demonstrated and developed. It is critical and a basic belief that teachers and librarians be closely involved in supporting all students on their journeys

Display books facing out and grouped by genre, as seen in popular bookstores.

through self-selection. After all, much time is devoted to the teaching of reading while very little time is dedicated to instructing these young readers on the importance of the selection process. To be successful, students need ample time to experience this actual learning.

Through PIE, our 21st century learners remember, understand, apply, analyze, evaluate, and create as they participate in self-selection. Here's how:

Remembering: Students recall the titles and genres they have chosen. Although they are not asked to memorize for PIE, students do keep a record of books chosen and read. PIE folders help to keep track of library maps, photographs of genre displays, CAT (call letters, author, title) slips, and story element summaries (SES).

Understanding: Students must explain ideas or concepts in PIE. They formulate questions to describe the kind of books they are seeking. They will soon locate and select books in the library and later contribute to discussions by explaining and summarizing what they have read.

Applying: Students use the information from PIE in new ways by choosing books recommended by others and later writing about the story elements found therein.

Analyzing: Students distinguish among the different parts of the library and the types of genre represented on the shelves. They compare and contrast one book with another as they choose to examine and distinguish by questioning if a certain book is the choice that is best for them.

Evaluating: Students may come to realize that their choice was not a good one and will always have the opportunity to select another book for PIE. As they listen to classmates' summaries and teacher or librarian book chats, they also formulate opinions for future book choices.

Creating: As a result of PIE, students create new points of view. They construct new meanings and develop a deeper sense of what real reading is. Throughout the year, students also design a simple way to feature a character, showcase a setting, or reenact a favorite scene to extend their learning to introduce their peers to the books they have enjoyed.

By placing independent self-selection at the center of PIE, our 21st century students will eventually ascend Bloom's taxonomy and distinguish one genre from another while also evaluating appropriate readability levels. It won't be long before students begin to understand that their eyes may have been bigger than their stomachs and that checking out the thickest book in the library does not guarantee that it will be their best choice for PIE. Students are on a daily quest to examine and reevaluate their own book choices to seek the one that is ultimately the best choice for them. Finally, these book choices, some taking more time than others, are then celebrated during classroom discussion meetings.

By using various PIE charts (see Appendix A), students are not overwhelmed with too many choices at once. Each PIE serves specific slices of genre to provide a framework for developing a taste for each flavor. At all times, it is the student who will decide which book

Have a plan and make good choices by using the library's OPAC.

Don't forget to check out what's just been returned to the library cart.

to select for PIE. The teacher may rename the slices to fit better with a basal text or other curriculum needs. Keep in mind the importance of beginning with only four slice PIES and then eventually increasing to eight slices.

What to Choose?

The librarian and teacher introduce students to the eight genres of PIE in a genre overview lesson. (See the PIE-to-Go Resources in Appendix A.) These are a collaborative lessons between the librarian and teacher which may be adapted to introduce one, some, or all genres together. Time is a factor, but future lessons may be scheduled over several weeks as needed. Teachers have the option of deciding which PIE to serve first and in which sequence. Folklore and graphic novels are also genres that may be substituted if desired.

- The first four-piece PIE includes realistic fiction, fantasy fiction, biography, and historical fiction.

- The second four-piece PIE includes nonfiction, science fiction, adventure/mystery fiction, and poetry.

- The eight-piece PIE includes realistic fiction, fantasy fiction, biography, historical fiction, science fiction, adventure/mystery fiction, poetry, and nonfiction (informational).

Toward the end of the year, the teacher may want to give students the option of creating a final PIE that includes the student's four favorite genres.

To facilitate better collaboration during PIE overview lessons, discussions, and future book chats, the teacher and librarian may want to refer to the following genre descriptions below to acquire a common genre vocabulary. Word clouds, posters, photos of book covers, or characters in digital picture frames may also be featured near each genre display to remind students, teachers, volunteers, and library staff of the characteristics of each.

- **Realistic fiction:** Could happen, believable, ordinary people in ordinary settings, often school-related, problems with resolutions, fast-paced action, everyday life, conflicts, common clothing, familiar character traits, characters may remind you of someone you know

  Meet realistic fiction characters: Examples include Clementine, Ramona, Beezus, Amber Brown, Judy Moody, Stink, Cobblestreet Cousins, Jenny Archer, Animal Ark, Fudge, Horrible Harry, Cody, Marvin, Junie B., Ever Ready Freddy, Grace, the Babysitter's Club, Horrid Henry, and Ivy and Bean

  Meet realistic fiction authors: Examples include Andrew Clements, Barbara Park, Beverly Cleary, Matt Christopher, Ben Baglio, Paula Danziger, Dan Gutman, Patricia Reilly Giff

- **Fantasy fiction:** Major events can't really happen, unrealistic story elements, animals that talk, battles between good and evil, impossible strategies, problems solved with magic, supernatural powers, make-believe adventures set in familiar or unfamiliar places, suspension of reality

  Meet fantasy fiction characters: Examples include Harry, Ron, Hermione, Bilbo Baggins, Gandolf, Charlie, James, Dorothy, Artemis, Eragon, Rainbow Magic Fairies

  Meet fantasy fiction Authors: Examples include Roald Dahl, J. R. R. Tolkein, J. Patrick Lewis, J. K. Rowling, L. Frank Baum, Eoin Colfer, Ursula LeGuin, Christopher Paolini, Tony DeTerlizzi, KateMcMullan, and Tony Abbott

- **Historical fiction:** Events may have happened; historically accurate; realistic fiction set in historical past; language that reflects the past; realistic characters; real events are mixed with fictional events; conflict, drama, clothing, foods, and prices all reflect the past

  Meet historical fiction characters: Examples include Meg, Jo, Beth, Amy, Josefina, Addy, Kirsten, Felicity, Molly, Samantha, Laura, and Sam the Minuteman

  Meet historical fiction authors: Examples include Alexander Dumas, Louisa May Alcott, My America series authors, Dear America series authors, Kathryn Lasky, Valerie Tripp, Laura Ingalls Wilder, and Alice Dalgliesh

- **Science Fiction:** Authors ask what if?; events happen in near or distant future; solve problems with scientific data or technology; robots; superheroes; outer space; based on scientific facts; three types: mind control, tomorrow's world, or survival; events are possible; characters may act like scientists; scientific point of view; setting may exist after a nuclear explosion or crash; new dimension in spaces and time; transformations; regenerate; clone; brain functions; weapons

<u>Meet science fiction characters:</u> Examples include Franny K. Stein, Captain Underpants, Ricky Riccotta, Weird Planet, Spider-man, McGrowl, Darth Vader, Jedi Knights, Animorphs, Melvin Beederman, Babymouse, Katie Kazoo, Ordinary Boy, Alex, Space Dog, aliens, avatars, clones, and robots

Meet science fiction Authors: Examples include Dav Pilkey, Jim Benton, Greg Trine, William Boniface, Frank Asch, Nancy Krulik

- **Mystery/Adventure fiction:** A story about a problem that needs to be solved without the use of magic, clues dropped throughout, realistic characters, believable solution, some distractions along the way, sometimes a first-person narrator, puzzling, reader is often questioning

  <u>Meet mystery/adventure fiction characters:</u> Examples include Jack, Annie, Cam, Jigsaw, Nate, Nancy, Clues Brothers, and Geronimo

  Meet mystery/adventure fiction authors: Examples include Carolyn Keene, David Adler, Marjorie Sharmat, James Preller, and Ron Roy

- **Non-fiction Informational:** Facts, photographs, illustrations, table of contents, glossary, index, specific topic, captions, diagrams, bold print, actual events, true, real people, real animals, real discoveries

  <u>Meet non-fiction informational subjects:</u> Examples include snakes, bats, dogs, cats, planets, penguins, rainforests, faraway countries, lions, foxes, sharks, bears, endangered animals, and parts of the human body

- **Biography:** Author tells about a real person, offers a timeline of important life's events, contains details of one's life story, photographs, index, table of contents

  <u>Meet biographical characters:</u> Examples include presidents, explorers, artists, sports heroes, authors, and inventors

  Meet biography authors: Such as Matt Christopher's At the Plate With—Mark Maguire, On the Halfpipe With . . ., or the Who Was series of famous people.

- **Poetry:** Plays with language, rhythm, rhyme, brings out emotions, often humorous, exaggerations, available in many forms (cinquain, haiku, alliteration, concrete, tanka, limericks)

  Meet poets: Examples include Silverstein, Florian, Prelutsky, Lansky, Dickinson, Frost, Hoberman, Viorst, Livingston, and Ciardi

A sampling of titles and authors from each of the above genres is available in the PIE-to-Go Resources in Appendix A.

Collaborative Practice: How to Choose?

How can we help each student to choose a book given this wide range of possibilities? It's a team approach.

Top Two Ways for Teachers and Librarians to Guide the Self-Selection Process

1. **Book Chats:** Schedule and share

One of the most important collaborative practices to schedule throughout the year are the book chats. These are short sessions (30–40 minutes) scheduled throughout the first half of the year and are facilitated by the librarian and supported by the classroom teacher. One genre is introduced per book chat in the library.

- Collaborate on the genre to be introduced and the current needs of the students.

- The librarian selects approximately 8–10 books from the featured genre that vary in reading level, interests, and authors and creates Star Review Forms. (See PIE-to-Go Resources.)

- The librarian gathers props and previews author websites.

- When writing plans for each book chat, the librarian should be sure to reference story element terms such as plot, character, and setting so that students become familiar with them.

- On the day of the book chat, librarian reserves a cozy corner of the library where all students are comfortable.

- The librarian delivers the book chat and maintains a list of the titles that were previewed for the teacher, students, and library volunteers to post in the library.

See PIE-to-Go Resources section for a sample book chat lesson plan.

Although it is recommended to read every book you preview in a book chat, if you find yourself short of time in preparing for these book chats, consult any of these great resources for helpful hints and popular book chat scripts.

PA Young Readers Choice Award (http://www.psla.org/grantsandawards/scripts .php4): New books are featured every year, and past nominees' booktalks are archived. Visit other state associations for their Young Readers Choice Award Programs, too.

Nancy Keane (http://nancykeane.com/booktalks) is a book goddess whose well-organized site will you help you create booktalks that are quick and simple.

IRA (International Reading Association's electronic journal hosted by Denise Johnson; http://www.readingonline.org/electronic/elec_index.asp?HREF=/electronic/webwatch/ book_talks/ features booktalk podcasts, bookfomercials, and even booktalks using imovie)

Podcasts (http://classroombooktalk.wikispaces.com)

2. **Strategies for choosing books at the appropriate level**

After listening to a book chat, students may begin to wonder how they will know if a book is the right choice for them. Remind students that good readers use different tactics and take their time to browse through several books before making a final selection at the correct level of difficulty.

a. One strategy found to be helpful is the "Meet and Greet" rule.

- Open the book to any page and with an open hand, wave "Hello" to the book.

- Read the first sentence aloud and for each unknown word, they put down one finger.

- Check this criteria to see if the book is a good fit.

0–1   Thumb down—the book is a great fit.

2   fingers down—the book is OK

3   fingers down—the book is getting difficult and you may need help with this book

4   fingers down—you will definitely need help with this book

5   fingers down—wave good-bye to this book for now (not forever) and say "Hello" to another

Book is OK Graphic

b. Model and teach students the value of previewing a book by reading the teaser that is found on the inside jacket flap or back cover. Reading the teaser will help the child determine both readability and interest.

c. Encourage students to use the "Ask Three Classmates Before Me" strategy before asking the librarian and teacher for help. This is a great way to get students talking to each other about their favorite book choices and their location in the library.

Fifteen Ways for Teachers to Help Students Self-Select Books

1. Form a partnership with your school librarian. He or she will become your direct connection to resources, research, ideas, and answers to your many questions.

2. Keep a variety of book titles in your classroom library from the current genre of emphasis. The public library, book clubs, garage sales, and student books from home will help, too.

3. Establish student classroom librarians to help with errands to and from the school library.

4. Read aloud picture books for an excellent way to build familiarity with the genre and to reinforce the characteristics of each rather than as actual choices for PIE. (See the PIE-to-Go Resources in Appendix A.)

5. Keep a classroom binder of scanned book covers of favorite classroom PIE books in alphabetical order by author or Dewey classification. Label each with call letters to assist students in locating them in the library.

6. Try not to miss a day of reading aloud to your students. (See PIE-to-Go Resources Section for Suggested Read-Alouds.) Be sure there's a chapter book going all year long to make those daily connections to genre and PIE story elements. These read-alouds will also spark future PIE choices by the same author. Routinely point out the author's last name and corresponding call letters on the book spines so your students may record these details on their "Books I Want to Read" sheets to help students locate them again in the future. (See PIE-to-Go Resources Section.) Also be sure to mention whether this book came from the school library, classroom library, public library, or perhaps belonged to you as a child. Jim Trelease (1992, 2001) continues to be a valued source for read-alouds and has offered thousands of recommendations over the years. His website (http://www .trelease-on-reading.com) also features much research on the importance of reading-aloud.

7. Bookmark websites such as the ones suggested below on classroom computers to open even more windows to those choices for PIE that are available outside the walls of your school.

Book Adventure (http://www.bookadventure.org) is a free reading motivation program for children in grades K to 8. Children create their own book lists from more than 7,000 recommended titles. Book Adventure was created by and is maintained by Sylvan Learning. It also includes a Teacher's Lounge and Parent Place.

Book Hive (http://www.plcmc.org/bookhive) is an award-winning guide to children's literature thanks to the Public Library of Charlotte and Mecklenburg County. This site truly has it all, including student-written reviews, podcasts, recommendations, and even opportunities for students to become authors themselves.

Hedgehog Books (http://www.hedgehogbooks.com), led by Vanya Jackowski, is supported by teachers who believe strongly that reading aloud to children will set them on a lifelong journey of learning and success. The website has lots of teacher reviews and the ability to search by title, author, or book characters. Top 10 lists include read-alones and read-alouds. The newsletters have not been updated since 2004.

Kidsreads' (http://www.kidsreads.com/bookertworm.asp) extensive author address list can help your students write to famous authors. There are polls, books in a series, author interviews, and even a "Books to Movies" section. Kidsreads is one of best places on the Internet for kids to find awesome new book reviews, author interviews, and special features on great books for all ages. There are also new trivia games, word scrambles, and incredible contests every month!

The Stacks for Kids (http://www.scholastic.com/kids/stacks/index.asp) is a very appealing site created by Scholastic for kids and their books. Books are listed by genre with

reviews that appear as you mouse over them. Also included are plenty of games, a Guess the Book trivia blog, puzzles, quizzes, author interviews, website links, and more!

Read Kiddo Read is (http://readkiddoread.com) James Patterson's new site dedicated to making kids readers for life.

8. Bookmark the URLs of your school library's OPAC, statewide or regional library access systems such as Access Pennsylvania's Power Library, to gain access to more PIE choices on all classroom computers.

9. Make daily genre connections with your basal reading series for extensions on all levels.

10. Organize classroom book baskets by genre to support future PIE selections.

11. Stay informed about the importance of self-selected reading. Visit a conference, attend a workshop, subscribe to a new educational e-newsletter, and read articles by professional researchers (e.g., Krashen, 2004, 2008; Krashen, Lee, & McQuillan, 2008; Loertscher & Woolls, 1999, 2002, 2005) who conduct valid literacy research. Or better yet, conduct some research of your own!

12. Ask, "What are you reading?" often and connect books to daily conversations for text-to-text, text-to-self, and text-to-world connections. Encourage books and their characters to be mentioned as part of your daily or weekly classroom meetings.

13. Join or start your own teacher book club to share children's titles with the teachers in your school. Or make it a part of grade-level team meeting discussions to find out what your coworkers are reading. Go online with Library Thing (http://www .librarything.com) or Good Reads (http://www.goodreads.net) or Shelfari, (http:// www.shelfari.com) to join discussion threads with hundreds of others. Posting your favorites to a social network will also get you connected with those who share your passion for children's literature.

14. Invite guest readers such as parents, principals, school helpers, special area teachers, local celebrities, or community helpers to come to the class each week as a "Mystery Reader" to read a picture book related to the current genre of emphasis. Keep a list of suggested titles handy to avoid duplicates. (See the PIE-to-Go Resources Section for PIE with Picture Books.)

15. Keep communication lines open with the parents of your students to learn how their children are enjoying or perhaps struggling with their PIE books at home.

Fifteen Ways for Librarians to Help Students Self-Select Books

1. Define yourself as a R4L (Reading for Life) Librarian and make purposeful contributions to your school's reading initiatives. Communicate, cooperate, and collaborate with classroom and special area teachers.

2. Build a library wiki, blog, or website complete with connections to pictures, polls, links to favorite authors, and your own electronic card catalog.

```
Call letters_____

Author's last name_____

Title_____
```

Figure 3.1 Call letters, Author, Title slip.

3. Set up your library in such a way that it promotes easier self-selection of PIE choices.

   • Provide accessible and informative displays of books according to genres.

   • Find ways to display various books facing out as is commonly done in popular bookstores.

   • Label the genre displays clearly.

   • Photograph display areas in the library to place within a floor-plan map to serve as a reference in student PIE folders.

   • Affix genre spine labels to books and mark shelves with shelf labels to denote larger genre sections. Stickers are available from suppliers such as Demco and Highsmith.

4. Customize your library's OPAC, online public access system, with features, buttons, links, and maps to help students locate books of various genres and interests.

5. Teach teachers and students how to use the library's OPAC. If it is Web based, introduce students and teachers to remote access from home and supply them with plenty of CAT slips (Figure 3.1).

6. Attend a PTA meeting to present and demonstrate how families can also obtain access to your library's OPAC from home.

7. Read and collaborate frequently with teachers, students, "public librarians" and community members to keep the PIE program fresh. Consider facilitating an after-school Teacher Book Club to discuss great finds for suggestions to students. Members may read the same title or mix up the reading list with high, medium, and lower level recommendations. Post suggestions to a wiki or to online sites such as Goodreads (http://www.goodreads.com) or Library Thing (http://shelfari.com) where members may rate and review their favorite books.

8. Instruct library volunteers in the physical arrangement of the library with a map as it relates to the PIE program (Figure 3.2). Offer a formal training session in your library to offer ways for volunteers to help students find what they are looking for. Repeat as needed throughout the year.

9. Offer one-on-one reader guidance to your students as often as possible by asking the right interview questions. "What was the last book you read that you really enjoyed? What was it you liked the most about that book?" Help students to articulate. Many

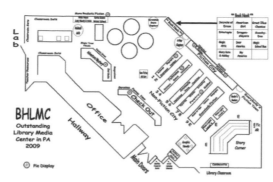

Figure 3.2 Library map (Used with permission of Amy Shope, library aide, Bower Hill Library Media Center, Peters Township School District, Venetia, PA.).

do not really know what kind of book they want. Short? Long? Pictures? Size of font? Boy or girl characters? "Do you want a book that makes you laugh?" Remind them to read the teaser, book jacket, and flap and to check the spine label for stickers. Meet and Greet books together when possible.

10. Form a partnership with your principal and parent–faculty club to showcase your schoolwide efforts. Co-chair your Book Fair and label Book Fair displays with matching PIE genre descriptions and provide parents with Classroom Wish Lists of suggested titles for PIE. Plan a Family Literacy Night with read-alouds, storytellers, book-related fun, and a chance for students to really show their parents around the library and allow parents to check out favorite books from your collection. Serve PIE for dessert or pizza PIE for a snack!

11. Attend conferences, workshops, and videoconferences to stay current and subscribe to listservs such as the American Association of School Librarians (aaslforum@ala.org), Keystone Technology Integrators (keystone@bucksiu.org), and the Commonwealth of Pennsylvania School Libraries (schools@hslc.org), where you will keep abreast of the latest research for our 21st century learners. Keep up with your professional reading, too.

12. Orient and reorient the students throughout the year with scavenger hunts in the library to check for understanding of the locations of PIE genre displays and guide words that lead them to favorite authors and nonfiction sections.

13. When resources are limited, librarians should consider purchasing multiple copies of highly popular titles in paperback to meet the needs of hungry readers. Purchasing books in a series is another good use of resources. Purchasing a variety of titles from a specific author also builds a strong collection. Interlibrary loans, public libraries, books from home, book fairs, warehouse sales, and grants such as Dollar General Youth Literacy Grant and AASL Innovative Reading Grant are viable alternatives when funds are limited.

14. Provide teacher and student surveys to plan ahead for future needs and purchases for PIE.

15. Assess your library's collection for a variety of genres, new and classic titles, levels of difficulty, and frequency of circulation. Follett, Perma Bound, and other book companies offer services to quickly analyze your collection online.

Top Ten Ways for Students to Self-Select Books

1. Practice the Meet & Greet Rule with every book.

2. Have a plan for book selection.

3. Use time wisely in the library and classroom.

4. Use the OPAC, wiki, and other electronic resources to help with the search.

5. When stumped, ask three classmates for help before seeking out an adult.

6. Think of good questions to ask the teacher, librarian, library staff, and parent volunteers about choices for PIE.

7. Read the teasers on jacket flaps and covers to learn more about a PIE book before checking it out.

8. Review Star Reviews for future PIE choices.

9. Use online resources such as those listed below to discover more recommendations for PIE from students around the globe.

    Scholastic (http://www.scholastic.com/kids/stacks/index.asp)

    Spaghetti Book Club (http://www.spaghettibookclub.org)

    The Book Hive (http://www.plcmc.org/bookhive

    Kids Reads (http://www.kidsreads.com/clubs)

    Al Roker's Book Club for Kids (http://today.msnbc.msn.com/id/33436633/ns/today-today_books)

    Oprah's Book Club for Kids (http://www.oprah.com/article/oprahsbookclub/kidsreadinglist/pkgkidsreadinglist/20080805_orig_kids_6_9)

10. Listen to student podcasts (http://classroombooktalk.wikispaces.com)

Top Ten Ways for Parents to Help Their Children to Self-Select Books

1. Encourage DEAR (Drop Everything and Read) Time at home and engage your child in conversation about the books they are reading for PIE.

2. Visit the public library often and be sure to let your child sign up for their own library card to access more books for PIE. Don't miss out on summer reading programs and special weekend events.

3. Read aloud to your child and ask him or her about the story elements. Consult available parenting resources such as Mem Fox's book, *Reading Magic*, and her

website (http://www.memfox.net or http://childrensbooks.about.com/cs/forparents/fr/readingmagic.htm).

4. The following sites/blogs are also great to mark as Favorites or to follow on Facebook or Twitter.

   Reading is Fundamental (http://www.rif.org/parents/)

   Jim Trelease (http://www.trelease-on-reading.com/parent-reading-brochure.html)

   Planet Esme (http://planetesme.blogspot.com)

   Jon Scieszka (http://www.guysread.com/)

   James Patterson (http://readkiddoread.com)

5. Volunteer in the classroom or school library.

6. Keep books in the car and ask your child to read aloud while you are driving or waiting for appointments.

7. Be sure your child has a book light, bookmarks, and a place for plenty of books.

8. Ask to see your child's PIE folder at least twice a week.

9. Visit bookstores together and ask your child for gift suggestions for friends and relatives based on favorite PIE books.

10. Praise your child for his or her accomplishments.

After students have made the appropriate book choices, they are ready to read their new selections. This next step of the PIE program, "Reading the Book," is an essential component toward helping students grow into readers. Although it seems obvious that reading books is important, the next chapter will highlight the significance of providing time for independent reading each day and developing the reading habit in young learners.

References

American Association of School Librarians. *Standards for the 21st-Century Learner*. Chicago: American Library Association, 2007. Also available online: http://www.ala.org/aasl/standards.

American Library Association and the Association for Educational Communications and Technology (1998). *Information Literacy Standards for Student Learning*. Chicago, IL: ALA.

Bloom BS (ed.) (1956). *Taxonomy of Educational Objectives, the classification of educational goals—Handbook 1: Cognitive Domain*. New York: McKay.

Fox, M. (2008). *Reading Magic*. New York: Mariner Books.

Krashen, S. (2008). *The Case for Libraries and Librarians*. Invited Paper, submitted to the Obama-Biden Education Policy Working Group.

Krashen, S. (2004). *The Power of Reading*, 2nd ed. Portsmouth, NH: Heinemann Publishers and Libraries Unlimited.

Krashen, S., Lee, S. Y., & McQuillan, J. (2008). *Is the Library Important?* Presented at the 37th annual meeting of the International Association of School Librarianship, Berkeley, CA.

Lance, Keith C, Linda Welborn, & Christine Hamilton-Pennell (1993). *The Impact of School Library Media Centers on Academic Achievement.* Castle Rock, CO: Hi Willow Research and Publishing (available from LMC Source at http://www.lmcsource.com under research).

Lance, Keith C., Marcia J. Rodney, & Christine Hamilton-Pennell (2000). *How School Librarians Help Kids Achieve Standards: The Second Colorado Study.* San Jose, CA: Hi Willow Research and Publishing, 2000.

Loertscher, D., & Woolls, B. (2002). *Information literacy: A review of the research: A guide for practitioners and researchers.* Castle Rock, CO: Hi Willow Research and Pub.

Loertscher, D., & Woolls, B. (2005). *The Whole School Library Handbook.* Castle Rock, CO: American Library Association.

Loertscher, D. V., & Woolls, B. (1999). Do library media programs contribute to academic achievement? Consider the evidence. *Knowledge Quest* Jan–Feb:24–26.

Trealease, J. (2001). *Hey! Listen to This: Stories to Read Aloud.* New York: Penguin Books.

Trealease, J. (2001). *The Read-Aloud Handbook*, 5th ed. New York: Penguin Books.

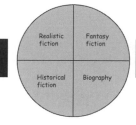

Chapter 4

Reading the Book

After selecting their books, students are asked to begin to read their stories. In the PIE (Personalized, Independent Enrichment) program, this simple step is given great consideration and intentional planning to ensure that students have time to read each day. Silent reading of PIE books is part of the daily reading program, and in PIE classrooms, seeing students reading independently is not unusual. To find time in a busy day, independent reading often needs to take the place of a workbook page or other seatwork. Krashen (2004) reports research findings that independent reading can positively impact children's reading comprehension and vocabulary development. In our simple terms, kids who read for fun become better readers. When students acquire a taste for reading independently, they tend to develop a habit that lasts a lifetime.

Collaborative Practice between the Teacher and the Librarian

Daily Reading in the Classroom

Teachers and librarians can provide many opportunities for daily independent reading of PIE books:

- Assign independent reading as morning work for students upon arrival.

- Combine snack time as silent reading time.

Meeting and greeting a book with five fingers up says you've found a great book to read independently!

- Both the teacher and librarian should read a book of their choice while students are reading silently. Modeling this behavior is a powerful motivator to reluctant readers.

- Make independent reading part of the assigned seatwork when working with small groups.

- Assign independent PIE reading as part of students' nightly homework.

- Stress and model the importance of silent reading time every day. Be sure that students see the teacher reading children's literature for pleasure, too. In doing so, teachers will be able to contribute more to class discussions.

Monitoring Students' Reading Progress

- Students should record their reading progress in their weekly reading logs. Teachers can review the logs to check for progress and encourage students to bring their logs to the library for the librarian to review as well.

- Teachers and librarians can also monitor students' understanding of the books they are reading based on their comments when they describe what they have read so far.

- Teachers and librarians should check to be sure that students have chosen books at the appropriate level of difficulty. Students who are choosing books that are too easy

Getting to know a book by spending some uninterrupted time inside the first chapter.

or too difficult for them should be monitored closely. Teachers and librarians should provide suggestions and support with the selection process if necessary.

Encouraging Reluctant PIE Readers

Students who are not making adequate weekly progress through their PIE books may need additional support and guidance. These strategies can address this problem:

- Reluctant readers are often unable to make appropriate book choices, and they do not care to ask for assistance with this task. Schedule a weekly time for the librarian to work one on one with these students to ask questions about their interests and to spend time discussing their book choices. This in-depth assistance will pay huge rewards later toward developing more positive attitudes about reading.

- Teachers and librarians can help "jump start" a book for students who have trouble getting into a story. After making a book choice, the teacher or librarian can read aloud a few pages or the first chapter to hook the reader into wanting to read more. Then the teacher or librarian can alternate reading aloud pages with the student until the student is ready to read the book independently.

- Touch base several times through the week with reluctant students to monitor their progress and ask questions about their book.

- Build a relationship with the parents of these readers to help gain their support with the PIE program.

Perhaps most important is that teachers and librarians communicate their own passion for reading to their students. When teachers talk about their own fondness of books, students readily adopt the same attitude and grow to love books, too.

Reference

Krashen, S. (2004). *The Power of Reading*, 2nd ed. Portsmouth, NH: Heinemann Publishers and Libraries Unlimited.

Chapter 5

Writing About the Book

Writing about the elements of a story helps students develop a deeper understanding of what they read. After students are finished reading their PIE (Personalized, Independent Enrichment) book, they are asked to write about the characters, setting, and plot through the use of a story element guide (SEG). The SEG is very specific and helps students think and write about the most important details of the story.

Students use the SEG to help them formulate their ideas in their composition notebooks to write a story elementary summary (SES). In the creation of this SES, students begin to think critically about their books. When students create an SES:

- It forces them to go beyond the memorization of facts and to examine their own understanding of the story (Harvey & Goudvis, 2000).

- It provides practice in helping the students to break down the parts of a story.

- It helps students learn how to include the big ideas and the most significant details, including the problem and solution.

In writing the SES, students practice the thinking and writing skills that will empower them to become independent learners.

Another key component of the SES is the "make a connection" portion. Students are asked to make one of three different types of connections to the book they read: text-to-text, text-to-world, or text-to-self connections (Keene & Zimmerman, 1997).

- **Text-to-text connection:** Students think critically about events from a book they read previously and make informed connections to the book they just read.

- **Text-to-world connection:** Students use their experiential knowledge to associate what they know about the world around them and the books they read.

- **Text-to-self connection:** Students consider events that have happened to them and link them with the experiences of the characters in the books.

When students make connections to what they read, it helps them to make the characters come alive and deepens their understanding of the author's purpose.

Collaborative Practice

Steps to Helping Students Write an SES

Teacher's Role

1. Modeling is a great first step in teaching an SES. This is best accomplished by reading aloud a picture book from a particular genre. It is important to choose a book that demonstrates vivid characters, settings, and plots. Before reading, discuss the genre and what students should look for as the book is read. Ask them to pay particular attention to the characters, the setting, and the most important events in the story. After the teacher and students discuss the genre, it is time to introduce the SEG. Display the SEG on an overhead transparency or computer projector and share and discuss the parts of the SES that the students will create with the use of the SEG. It is important to go through the expectations carefully so that students fully understand how to follow the framework.

   Afford students the opportunity to work in small groups to list the characters, setting, and main events of the story read aloud to them in sequential order. Also ask them to write down the problem and the solution. After each group has accomplished this task, the teacher should model the process of creating an SES. Modeling and collaborating among students and teachers helps ensure that the process is being learned. (A more detailed lesson plan may be found in the PIE-to-Go Resources in Appendix A.)

2. Students are given a composition notebook in which to write their Story Element Summaries for the year. They use the SEG as a framework to ensure they include the most critical parts. Throughout the year, as students write an SES, improvement will be evident. Be aware that it will take students time to master the art of writing, and patience and encouragement from the teacher are necessary to establish clear, well-written element summaries.

3. Teachers should note that there are four different types of Story Element Guides, which depend on the genre. The SEG used most often in the program is the one for fictional stories, which is used for realistic fiction, fantasy, historical fiction, adventure/mystery, and science fiction. SEGs have been created specifically for the other three remaining genres: biography, poetry and nonfiction informational.

4. Modeling how to write meaningful connections to the story is another critical component to teaching students how to write an SES. As students read, they naturally make connections to themselves and the world around them. Teaching students how to make quality connections to the literature they are reading helps deepen their understanding of the stories they read. As teachers model quality connections, students will begin to see how the books they read relate to the world around them.

> **Text-to-self connection:** Making a text-to-self connection allows students the opportunity to make a very personal correlation to what they are reading, and the information becomes important to them. With certain types of genre such as realistic fiction, students can make these connections easily. However, with other genre such as fantasy, students may struggle to think of a connection because the story is often not based in reality. In these situations, reminding students that they can think of a character's thoughts, actions, and feelings rather than events that may have occurred may be helpful.

> **Text-to-text connection:** This type of connection requires students to think about a story they have read previously and make a connection with the books they are currently reading. Ask students to think about how the books they are reading are similar to previous books they have read. Students may also connect two chapters of the same book and tell how a character may have changed. Making connections between texts helps children to think critically and use their prior knowledge to better understand each text.

> **Text-to-world connection:** This type of connection asks students to relate what they are reading to the world around them. They need to ask themselves questions such as, What does this remind me of that happens in the real world? How does this character remind me of someone in the real world? As students think about questions like these, they will begin to better understand how the world works. Teachers will also begin to see students make text-to-world connections in other curricular areas such as science and social studies.

Librarian's Role

1. Because the librarian is such an essential part of the PIE program, teachers and librarians should collaborate whenever possible to practice the understanding of the story elements. This will help facilitate the idea that the library plays an integral part in students' understanding of literature. The more practice students have using the story elements, the better their Story Element Summaries will become.

PIE Journals can also serve as valuable Data Notebooks.

Planning our weekly PIE assignments helps to keep us on track.

Looking over our story elements before meeting with our PIE group help us to recall our favorite points.

2. Librarians may invite students to share their SES with the library to be displayed where the book is currently shelved. As other students in the school view these summaries, they will be encouraged to want to check out the book.

3. Librarians may assist students in writing student reviews to appear in the library's Online Public Access Catalog (OPAC) in the "notes line" and read by fellow students as they search for future PIE books. This will motivate other students to want to participate.

References

Harvey, S. & Goudvis, A. (2000). *Strategies that work: Teaching comprehension to enhance understanding*. Portland, ME: Stenhouse.

Keene, E. & Zimmerman, S. (1997). *Mosaic of thought*. Portsmouth, NH: Heinemann.

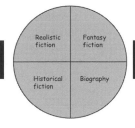

Chapter 6

Sharing the Book

In the third step of the PIE (Personalized, Independent Enrichment) program, sharing the book, students participate in a collaborative group to articulate their thoughts and ideas about the books they are reading. Specifically, the teacher or librarian and a small group of students meet and share their books with each other on a weekly basis. Providing common sharing time is frequently overlooked in many reading programs. As educators, we provide time to question students about the books and stories they have read, but we rarely facilitate a planned meeting time that is student led. In the PIE program, students meet in a small group with the teacher once a week to talk about the books they are reading and participate in informal conversations about their books.

This activity also helps to build a community of readers through shared literary experiences. The members of the PIE group become familiar with each member's book choices and look forward to hearing more about the stories each week. This community is extended into a deepened teacher–student relationship as students have the opportunity to converse with their teacher on a more personal basis.

Students share a common language when discussing their books. They speak effortlessly about the setting, the plot, the characters, and the conflicts they are facing. When the elements of the story are applied to the books the students are reading, the elements become natural and easy to understand.

When students are engaged in conversations about their books, their level of comprehension is heightened, creating a deeper understanding of the plot. It is often through the retelling of a story that children recognize how thoroughly they understand it. Through this sharing activity, teachers and school librarians can show students how to connect stories to their own personal experiences, other books they have read, and the world around them. Good readers make these connections naturally, but struggling readers often fail to see how one book connects to anything else. These connections are vital in helping students see the relevance of the books they are reading.

When books are shared among classmates, students become interested in checking out these particular books themselves. School librarians often comment on the increased circulation of specific titles that were recently shared in a PIE meeting. Students listen and discuss their favorite books and make both mental and actual notes to choose the books as future PIE selections when they get the opportunity. Students can record these notes about titles on the "Books I Want to Read" sheet in their folders. (See the PIE-to-Go Resources in Appendix A.)

Book sharing through the PIE program offers students the opportunity to practice many of the 21st century skills that educators recognize as being important to success. These include:

- Learning how to work cooperatively with students of different abilities and interests

- Working collaboratively with each other to share ideas about books through recommendations and reviews

Students are given many opportunities at the PIE table to practice good listening and speaking skills.

It's always a treat to be able to share what you've written with others!

Most importantly, both teachers and students find the book sharing sessions to be one of the highlights of their week. For teachers and librarians, these sessions are easy to conduct and rewarding to watch. For students, book sharing is an authentic experience as they develop into kids who love to read!

The classroom teacher is an active listener during PIE book sharing sessions and facilitates additional opportunities for further discussions throughout the day.

Chapter 7

The Collaborative Practice of Sharing Books

Both teachers and librarians share a role in facilitating this important step of the PIE (Personalized, Independent Enrichment) program, but teachers own many of the preliminary steps before the book sharing session begins.

Creating Book Sharing Groups

Teachers should build small groups of six to eight students, which can be either homogeneous or heterogeneous. Homogeneous groups offer many benefits. Students with comparable reading abilities often read books of similar levels of difficulty; this is advantageous because they are able to make recommendations of new titles to one another. Effort should be made to keep the group to a maximum number of eight students because this increases the opportunity for informal and open conversation.

Setting Up the Meeting Place

The area that is designated for the PIE meeting should be located in a quiet spot that is free from distractions. Some teachers use a table and chairs, and others meet with small groups in a circle on the floor. Teachers should be able to facilitate the PIE group while still keeping the rest of the class in view. It is important to keep all necessary PIE materials within reach of the meeting space to help the process flow smoothly.

Facilitating the Book Sharing Meeting

Although it may appear unstructured, there is a general routine that teachers can follow to facilitate a smooth and functional book sharing session. The steps of this procedure are listed below:

1. The teacher calls one group of students to the PIE area. They should bring all necessary items, including their pencils, PIE folders, and PIE books.

2. Students begin by reviewing their Weekly Assignment Sheet. (See the Weekly Assignment Sheet sample in PIE-to-Go Resources in Appendix A.) Next students update the Assignment Sheet by checking off the task(s) they will accomplish during the coming week. These tasks include choosing a new book, continuing to read a book, writing a story element summary (SES), or preparing a project upon completing an entire PIE. The completion of these Weekly Assignment Sheets serves to keep students on track and helps the teacher monitor individual progress. Additionally, it is an excellent communication tool for parents who wish to support their children in the PIE process.

3. After updating the Weekly Assignment Sheet, each child takes a turn sharing some information with the group. If the student is still reading the book, then he or she can give the group a short summary of the plot and let the group know if he or she is enjoying the book. Some students will be ready to read their SES for the group. Others may be ready to share a book project that they've completed over the past week. All students should take a turn updating the group with their weekly progress. Encourage students to bring the books they have read or are reading to the meeting. The teacher can set the book on a small tabletop easel while the student is speaking to help students focus on the highlighted book.

4. During this sharing time, it is helpful for the teacher to encourage other group members to join the conversation. Students do not typically have many opportunities during the school day to practice this type of discourse. It is for this reason that teachers need to cultivate the discussion skills that students need to participate in a book sharing session. Teachers may choose not to require students to raise their hands during the meeting. Instead, they can teach and expect students to use appropriate conversation manners and to ask deep questions of each other during the book sharing session. Encouraging students to ask rich follow-up questions of their classmates develops thinking skills as well. Students are expected to ask open-ended questions to stimulate discussion among group members. At the start of the year, students may need to use the book sharing question cards to help them ask better questions of their classmates. (See the book sharing questions in the PIE-to-Go Resources in Appendix A.) After these conversation skills are mastered, teachers find that students truly enjoy the informal and enriching climate of the book sharing sessions!

Conversation Rules for a Book Sharing Session

- Face the speaker and listen attentively.
- Speak without interrupting.

- Ask rich follow-up questions of each other.

- Stay on the topic that is being discussed.

- Be kind when giving a different opinion.

5. After everyone has had an opportunity to share their progress with the group, students pack up their materials and return to their seats. It is time for the teacher to meet with another group.

Helpful Tips to Ensure a Successful Book Sharing Session

1. Keep the atmosphere relaxed and fun! Students should look forward to PIE day and the opportunity to meet with their classmates.

2. Be sure to allow enough time for each group. Generally, 20 to 25 minutes should be sufficient for a group of six to eight students.

3. Insist on keeping the rest of the classroom quiet while the PIE group meets with the teacher. Additionally, teach students to postpone questions for the teacher until the group finishes a session. This is good opportunity for the other students to work on different PIE activities at their seats. These include:

- Reading their PIE book silently

- Writing an SES

- Visiting the library to look for another PIE book or accessing the library online through OPAC to fill out a CAT (call letters, author, title) slip (as shown in Chapter 3)

- Working on a PIE project

- Completing purposeful seatwork

4. A teacher might want to use a fishbowl approach to model the book sharing session with the class. He or she should choose a group that has mastered the elements of a book sharing session and have them sit in the center of the classroom. The other students should sit in a circle around the group. Then the model group along with the teacher will conduct a book sharing session for the others to observe. Periodically throughout the session, the teacher may want to stop and point out the aspects of the session that help to make it successful.

Refer to the following dialogue from a book sharing session to help capture the flavor of a successful meeting.

Teacher (T): Hi everyone! Let's get started by getting out your Weekly Assignment Sheet and decide what your plan will be for next week. Today's date is October 5. Please record that on your chart and then check off all of the tasks that you will do this coming week.

Sara: I am sure that I will be able to finish my book this week and also do a story element summary.

Sam: I am still reading my book. It has a lot of chapters!

Michael: I need to choose another book, and I think I am going to look for a good biography. Does anyone have any ideas?

Beth: Yeah. I read a great one on Thomas Edison. Do you want to read my story element summary?

Michael: Sure!

T: Okay. If you have all recorded your tasks for next week, then let's take turns talking about the books we are reading. Sara, why don't you begin?

Sara: Well, I am almost finished with my book. I read a lot this week. [She shows her Reading Log.] I have been reading *The Borrowers*. It is a really good book about these little people that live under the floorboards of a house!

T: Sara, can you read us one of your favorite parts of the story so far?

Sara: [Reads aloud from the book.]

[Some students get out their Books that I Want to Read sheets and write down the title and call number of the book.]

T: Great! I remember reading that book when I was in school! Thanks, Sara, Okay, Sam, you are next.

Sam: I am reading *Shredder Man*. It's about a boy that has been bullied and decides he is going to fight back. I like it because it sort of reminds me of something that happened to me in school last year. There was a kid on the bus who used to always call me names and push me around. I wish I had read this book last year!

Michael: I read a book called *The Monster's Ring* over the summer. It was about a boy who was being bullied, too! But it was fantasy because he turned into a were-wolf by turning a ring.

T: Sam, can I see your reading log? Looks like you will probably finish your book in another week or two. I am glad that you found a realistic fiction book that you are enjoying. Michael, you said you are looking for a good biography?

Michael: Yeah, I got one on Tiger Woods, but I returned it because I didn't really like it. It was a little hard for me to understand. I am going to try the one on Thomas Edison.

Beth: I can show you where it is in the library if you want. It was really interesting how he never gave up on his inventions. That reminds me of my brother when he is working on his science fair projects!

T: That's what good readers do—they choose books that they are going to enjoy. Sometimes you have to try a few before you find one that you really like. Biographies can be challenging. Remember to check with Mrs. O. in the library if you need some other ideas. She is always interested in what we are reading for PIE. We will be interested next week in finding out what you picked for your biography choice.

Beth: I am ready to read my story element summary on *Spiderwick*. [She reads her SES to the group.]

T: Well done, Beth! Anybody have any thoughts about this story?

Sam: That was my favorite *Spiderwick* book.

Sara: Me too, but I also love the *Field Guide*.

Michael: I never read them, but I am writing down the title for my next fantasy!

T: That was a great summary, Beth. You wrote the big ideas of the plot. I also enjoyed hearing your connections to other books. What genre are you looking for next?

Beth: I think I am going to look for a historical fiction, but I am going to wait until we have a book chat in the library with Mrs. O. so that I can get some good ideas.

T: Good idea! Okay, everybody, I really enjoyed hearing about what you are all reading. Head back to your seats and remember to keep reading this week! Would the next group please join me in the back of the room with your PIE folders?

The Librarian's Role in Book Sharing Sessions

Although teachers maintain primary responsibility for facilitating book sharing sessions in the classroom each week, librarians can play an important supporting role in this step as well. These strategies include:

1. Librarians may occasionally assist with the book sharing sessions by facilitating a group in the library. It may help to have the group sit in a prominent spot in the library so that other students can observe the activity while they are choosing their books. Talking about good books should be an informal and interesting experience that students enjoy. This positive feeling will generate interest among other teachers, students, and parents when they visit the library.

2. Librarians might also film a book sharing session in the classroom to use as an instructional tool for other teachers who are interested in starting the PIE program in their classroom.

3. A book sharing video may also be viewed on the schoolwide morning announcements for all of the students and teachers to view. This is a good way to preview some popular books and to encourage other students to read.

When teachers and librarians provide time for students to talk about their books in a purposeful way, it sends a powerful message to students that reading is an important and valuable lifelong activity.

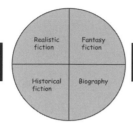

Chapter 8

Extending the Book

When students have completed an entire PIE, read all of the books, completed story element summaries (SES), and shared the summaries with their group, they are asked to extend their understanding of the story through an extension project. The purpose of the project is to:

- Create a project about their book that brings together all of the pieces of the novel into a product for others to experience.

- Build comprehension skills by bringing the story to life.

- Increase enjoyment of the book through creative expression.

- Advertise the book so others will want to read it.

Teachers and librarians need to provide practice helping students to think more deeply about the books they have read and how to share these thoughts creatively with others. When students create meaning from text through a project, they gain a deeper understanding of the story elements. In this process, the value of a good story is promoted and emphasized.

The Collaborative Practice of Extending Books

The Teacher's Role in Extending Books

Students are asked to do an extension activity or project after they complete an entire PIE. Specifically, after a student has read a book from all of the genres and completed an SES and shared it with the PIE group for each of these books, he or she is ready to do an extension project. Classroom teachers can provide many resources and opportunities for students to extend their understanding of a book. Extension projects can include any of the following:

- Plan creative dramatizations of favorite scenes.
- Create story advertisements to promote the book.
- Write a letter to the author.
- Create a new book cover.
- Write a sequel to the story.
- Write a prequel to the story.
- Read another story by the same author and tell about it.
- Do a puppet show with some of the characters from the book.
- Create a game board about the story.
- Dress up as one of the characters and read a dialogue from the book.
- Be a book critic and write a review of the book.
- Create a comic strip about the book.
- Build a diorama about a scene from the book.
- Create a poster of the book.
- Interview another person who read the book.
- Write a letter to the author.
- Write another chapter.
- Write a different ending.
- Create a timeline of the story events.
- Write a song about the book.

The School Librarian's Role in Extending Books

School librarians also play an important role in helping students to develop a deeper understanding of books through extension projects. This can be accomplished by finding a balance between traditional and innovative methods.

- Student projects can be displayed in the library next to the book that is being highlighted. This serves as an advertisement and invitation to both students and teachers to read the book. It also provides the school librarian with a visual example to refer to while offering book suggestions to new readers. Student projects on display also help a library become a learning commons where students talk about their books again, share opinions, and seek new knowledge. The librarian should also keep corresponding CAT (call letters, author, title) slips in supply next to all student projects to direct future readers to the book's location in the library.

- School librarians and classroom teachers can schedule a "Let's Connect Session," which is led by one student each week during the scheduled library time. The student should prepare a presentation that highlights one of the following connections:

  o Text-to-self

  o Text-to-world

  o Text-to-text

Extending the Book with Technology

Note to school librarians: Remember that even our youngest students are commonly referred to as "digital natives" and members of the "thumb generation." Talk to any one of them about their interests, and you will see that they are seeking the latest upgrades for their video games, social networks, and operating systems. By encouraging your students to use these new forms of technology with the PIE (Personalized, Independent Enrichment) program, not only will they enjoy innovative ways to creatively express themselves but they will also have a variety of opportunities to share what they have read with a much wider audience. Thanks to technology, their opinions, recommendations, and sources for new books can easily be broadcast outside and posted far beyond the classroom walls. Internet safety procedures should be modeled and reinforced at all times.

- Become a technology leader in your school and schedule mini lessons with students and teachers to highlight new technology as it becomes available. Wikis such as http://teachweb2.wikispaces.com/ provide new web 2.0 tools that will help to integrate technology throughout the school.

- Attend technology workshops on the local, state, and national levels. Keep one step ahead with free online tutorials suggested by your local school library association or other web 2.0 links, such as http://www.classroom20.com, http://mhmsmedia .wikispaces.com/, which offers school librarians the new tools for blogs, photos, and images, RSS and newsfeeds, tagging and technorati, wikis, online applications, podcasting, downloadable audio, and much more. Or get immediate help from librarians who Twitter by visiting Elementary Library Routines http://elementarylibraryroutines .wikispaces.com/

- A host of other tech resources to share with your staff may also be found at WebTools4U2Use (http://webtools4u2use.wikispaces.com/Presentation+Tools), and Atomic Learning (http://www.atomiclearning.com) provides educators with helpful online tutorials.

- Extend the book with tech templates.

PIE projects are a perfect way for students to develop, design, and imagine.

ReadWriteThink (http://www.readwritethink.org/student_mat/index.asp) offers a wealth of extension ideas where K to 12 students can create new book covers, bio cubes, acrostic poems, comics, and more. Simple templates help students fracture fairy tales, create mystery cubes, design postcards for favorite authors, create descriptive timelines, or even write like Geronimo Stilton by creating their own Doodle Splashes.

If you need help in implementing any of these technology extensions into your lesson plans, connect to Byrdseed Gifted Lessons (http://www.byrdseed.com/differentiator) for a simplified electronic template of project options.

Extend the Book by Podcasting Book Reviews

When kids get talking about books, they may find it hard to stop. One of the easiest ways to preserve this enthusiasm is through podcasting. Students can write and record their own book reviews and inspire others to read with a computer and a small microphone. There is a wonderful link from this website that directs teachers and students through the simple steps of podcasting. (See Learning in Hand at http://learninginhand.com/podcasting) and PodOmatic at (http://terryfreedman.podomatic.com.)

When your students believe they are ready to create a podcast, provide them with a template of what to include in their review. Background music, a possible teaser question, a drawing or photograph of the book's cover, and a script are several elements that need to be in place before recording. Your students also need to practice their podcasts often before producing them, which is an excellent way to improve reading fluency without the drudgery of reading aloud a passage that bears no positive connection to the reader. Students will also be more enthusiastic about recording their own words and will better understand the need to use expression when persuading, entertaining, or informing their audience. One of the best features of podcasts is that the students can quickly self-assess their own performance and redo it with a click. By posting these podcasts to a wiki, blog, or website, your students can even track their listeners with sites such as ClustrMaps (http://www.clustrmaps.com). Student produced podcasts can also be forwarded to Mom's cell phone, Dad's Blackberry, or Grandad's iPod.

To inspire your students, be sure to expose them to quality podcasting. The students of Willowdale Elementary in Omaha, Nebraska, produce a first-rate radio-talk program. They call it Radio Willow (http://millard.esu3.org/willow/radio) Imagine the possibilities of conducting Radio PIE from your very own school! It is also possible to retell favorite folktales such as Abiyoyo with podcasts that use musical sound effects like the students of General Wayne Elementary School in Malvern, PA. (http://www.gvsd.org/18872056133747577/podcasts/browse.asp?a=399&BMDRN=2000&BCOB=0&c=58382&18872056133747577Nav=|1479|&NodeID=2041).

Check out VoiceThread (http://www.voicethread), Photostory, and Audacity, Inc. (http://www.audacity.com) for additional free resources to extend PIE book reviews.

Extend the Book with Flip Cameras or Video Cameras

Record student performances of a PIE reader's theater or a puppet show based on a favorite scene in a PIE book. Or hold a press conference for a famous biography character and record the question-and-answer session. After building a diorama, students may want to zoom in and video each aspect while narrating. And students may want to take any of these projects one step further by editing and creating their own iMovie and posting it to SchoolTube (http://www.schooltube.com). Need equipment? Seek out grants or post your wishes on Digital Wish (http://www.digitalwish.com).

Use Skype (http://www.skype.com) to arrange a virtual author visit or to share your PIE extensions with students in other schools. Formulate your questions ahead of time as you would when writing a personal letter. Be sure to discuss arrangements with your technology coordinator or technician in advance. Check out Skype An Author Network (http://skypeanauthor.wetpaint.com/page/Directions+for+Teachers+%26+Librarians) for directions and a list of authors who Skype.

Extend the Book with Comics, Cartoons, and Animations

GoAnimate (http://www.goanimate.com) gives students the opportunity to create comic strips and animations of favorite book characters in a favorite scene in a brand new setting or to suggest a completely different ending to the book. Imagine Ramona meeting Captain Underpants or Jack and Annie landing in your own backyard.

Comic Life (http://www.comiclife.com) is an award-winning site where students can use their creativity to drag and drop speech bubbles over digital photos of themselves, book characters, book covers, or even scenes around the school. What might a biography of Abraham Lincoln say to Flat Stanley if both books were left on the playground together?

Extend the Book with a Digital Camera and these Sites

Flickr (http://www.flickr.com) is a photo sharing site that offers countless ways for students to be creative with photos. Students can use photographs to spell words for posters, and even add images to slides for visual storytelling. Another great link for educators who want to integrate technology into their lessons can be found at iLearnTechnology.

Big Huge Labs (http://www.bighugelabs.com) helps students create trading cards for PIE, design magazine covers, jigsaw puzzles, maps of a character's journey, or even add pizzazz to posters and presentations for PIE. The site has recently added a Big Huge Thesaurus, which is a great tool to help students expand their vocabulary and writing skills.

Extend the Book with these Presentation Sites

Animoto (http://www.animoto.com) helps you and your students create amazing PIE music videos.

Slide (http://www.slide.com) allows students to customize slideshows of favorite PIE Books.

Glogster (http://http://edu.glogster.com) introduces students to the possibilities of adding voice, images, and stickers to interactive posters and online scrapbooks. It is also possible to embed videos from SchoolTube into this resource.

Prezi (http://www.prezi.com) offers a simple way to interact live with your PIE presentations.

Students may also want to present their PIE author's website to the class by navigating and sharing its special components such as author interviews, trivia, booklists, and author tips for writing and by introducing classmates to games that connect kids with books and their characters. Visit KidsReads (http://www .kidsreads.com) to get started.

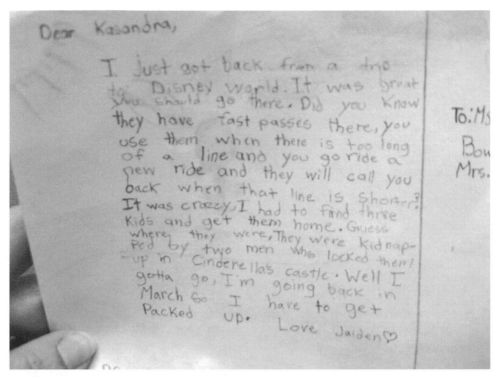

Producing a postcard from one book character to another gets students thinking about making predictions and inferences.

Capturing the setting on paper requires understanding, analysis, and transfer.

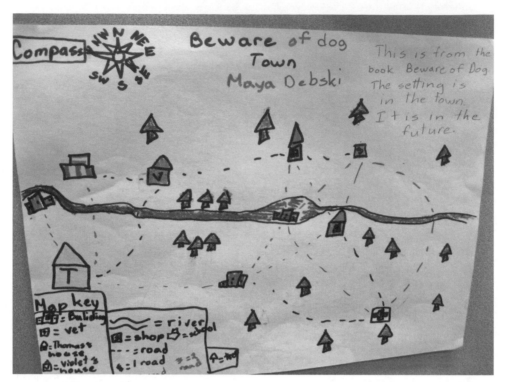

Planning a map of the book's setting also requires creativity and brings students to the top of the New Bloom's Taxonomy.

Book Extension Tips

- Remind students to keep their projects simple so as not to overshadow the book. Throughout all of the steps of PIE, it is important to emphasize that the book and the reader are the most critical components.

- Book projects can be displayed not only in the classroom and the library but also throughout the school in showcases, office displays, and on hallway bulletin boards. Projects might even be displayed in the cafeteria with captions such as:

  - Hungry for a Good Book?

  - Feed your Mind a Good Book

  - Treat Yourself to a Good Book

- Projects might be displayed in local businesses around the community, especially during Children's Book Week in the public library.

PIE-to-Go Resources

First Four Piece PIE

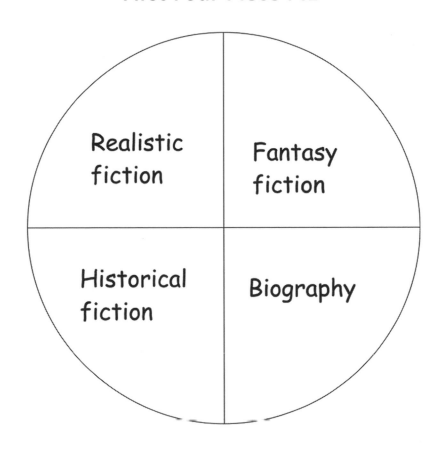

Name _____

Second Four Piece PIE

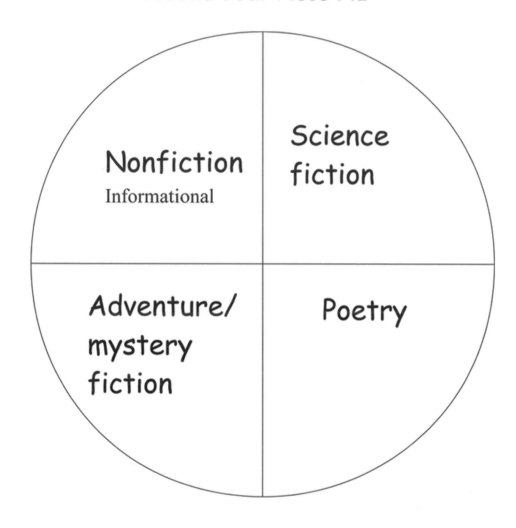

Name _____

Eight Piece PIE

Name _____

Weekly PIE Assignment Sheet

PIE Assignment Sheet							☑	Complete for Next Week		
								Be Ready to		
Mtg. Date	Genre		Read	Finish Reading	SES		Project	Share Book	Share Project

(Continued)

PIE Assignment Sheet					☑	Complete for Next Week		
						Be Ready to		
Mtg. Date	Genre		Read	Finish Reading	SES	Project	Share Book	Share Project

PIE Reading Log

Student _____

Book title _____

Author _____ Genre _____

Total number of pages _____ Call Letters _____

Date I started the book _____ Date I finished the book _____

I read:

Date _____ pages _____   Date _____ pages _____

Date _____ pages _____   Date _____ pages _____

Date _____ pages _____   Date _____ pages _____

Date _____ pages _____   Date _____ pages _____

Date _____ pages _____   Date _____ pages _____

Date _____ pages _____   Date _____ pages _____

Date _____ pages _____   Date _____ pages _____

Date _____ pages _____   Date _____ pages _____

Date _____ pages _____   Date _____ pages _____

Date _____ pages _____   Date _____ pages _____

Date _____ pages _____   Date _____ pages _____

Date _____ pages _____   Date _____ pages _____

Date _____ pages _____   Date _____ pages _____

Date _____ pages _____   Date _____ pages _____

Date _____ pages _____   Date _____ pages _____

Date _____ pages _____   Date _____ pages _____

 From *Personalized Reading: It's a Piece of PIE* by Nancy Hobbs, Kristen Sacco, and Myra R. Oleynik. Santa Barbara, CA: Libraries Unlimited. Copyright © 2011.

Books I Want to Read

Name: _____

CAT SLIP

Call letters _____   Genre _____

Author _____   Referred by _____

Title _____

_____

Name: _____

CAT SLIP

Call letters _____   Genre _____

Author _____   Referred by _____

Title _____

_____

Name: _____

CAT SLIP

Call letters _____   Genre _____

Author _____   Referred by _____

Title _____

Story Element Guide
for Fiction Books

Name   Date

Title:

Author:

Genre:

Characters: (List the main characters in the story)

Setting: (Write one sentence telling where the story takes place. Write one sentence telling if it happened in the past, present, or future.)

Plot:

Problem: (Write about the main problem of the book in a complete sentence.)

Solution: (Write about how the problem was solved in a complete sentence.)

Story events: (Write approximately 8 to 10 sentences telling what happened in the story—the beginning, middle, and end.)

Make a Connection: (Choose one of the following types of connections to write about. Remember to include both parts in your connection.)

TEXT-TO-TEXT—Make a connection between the story you are reading and another story you have read.

TEXT-TO-WORLD—Make a connection between the story you are reading and events that have happened in the world.

TEXT-TO-SELF—Make a connection between the story you are reading and experiences you have had in your own life.

Story Element Guide
for Biography

Name   Date

Title:

Author:

Genre:

Characters: (List the names of important people in the person's life.)

Setting: (Write one or two sentences telling where most of the important events in the story take place.)

Life events: (Write approximately 10 to 12 facts in paragraph form, telling what happened in the person's life in sequential order.)

Make a connection: (Choose one of the following types of connections to write about. Remember to include both parts in your connection.)

TEXT-TO-TEXT—Make a connection between the story you are reading and another story you have read.

TEXT-TO-WORLD—Make a connection between the story you are reading and events that have happened in the world.

TEXT-TO-SELF—Make a connection between the story you are reading and experiences you have had in your own life.

Story Element Guide
for Poetry

Name   Date

Title:

Author:

Genre:

Choose your two favorite poems. Be prepared to read the poems to your PIE group.

First Poem:

Title:

Author:

Characters: (List the main characters from the poem.)

Setting: (Write one sentence telling where the poem takes place.)

Plot: (Write a few sentences telling what the poem is about.)

Make a connection: (*TEXT-TO-SELF*—Connect the main idea of what happened in the poem to you or someone you know.)

Second Poem:

Title:

Author:

Characters: (List the main characters from the poem.)

Setting: (Write one sentence telling where the poem takes place.)

Plot: (Write a few sentences telling what the poem is about.)

Make a Connection: (*TEXT-TO-SELF*—Connect the main idea of what happened in the poem to you or someone you know.)

Presentation Guide for Nonfiction Informational Text

You have learned about something new! Now it is your turn to be the TEACHER and EXPERT! Use this outline to help you organize information about the subject discussed in your book. When presenting to your classmates, be creative! You can use a poster, props, experiments, and so on to share your new acquired information. Good luck and have fun!

Name: **Date:**

Title:

Author:

Genre:

Details: (Write specific details that you have learned about from reading this book to help you with your presentation.)

Explanation: Answer the following questions in complete sentences:

- Why did you choose this subject?

- What was the most interesting fact that you learned?

- How did you like this genre? What did you like about it?

- What didn't you like?

From *Personalized Reading: It's a Piece of PIE* by Nancy Hobbs, Kristen Sacco, and Myra R. Oleynik. Santa Barbara, CA: Libraries Unlimited. Copyright © 2011.

Story Element Summary: Fiction Sample

Name: **Date:**

Title: *Amazing Grace*

Author: Mary Hoffman

Genre: Realistic fiction

Characters: Grace, Nana, Mom, Natalie, and Raj

Setting: The story takes place in Grace's house, her school, her backyard, and the theater. It takes place in the present.

Plot:

Problem: Grace's schoolmates discourage her by telling her that she can't be Peter Pan in the class play.

Solution: Grace's mom and Nana encourage her and show her that she can do anything.

Story Events: Amazing Grace is a story about a girl who learns that she can do anything. Grace liked to act out the adventures told to her by her Nana. She tried hard to act out the scenes. So naturally, Grace was excited when she found out that her class was going to perform a play about Peter Pan and her teacher would have auditions for the parts. Grace wanted to be Peter Pan and knew that she could do it. So when she was told by other children that she couldn't play Peter because she was a girl and she was black, she felt discouraged. When she got home from school, her Nana took her to the theater to see the new Juliet from the play *Romeo and Juliet*. The star of the play was a young black girl just like Grace. Seeing this helped Grace to feel as if *she* could do anything. At the end of the story, Grace played the part of Peter Pan in the class play, and everyone told her that she made a wonderful Peter Pan.

From *Personalized Reading: It's a Piece of PIE* by Nancy Hobbs, Kristen Sacco, and Myra R. Oleynik. Santa Barbara, CA: Libraries Unlimited. Copyright © 2011.

Text-to-Self Connection:

When I was young, my brothers once told me that I couldn't play baseball with them and their friends because I was a girl. I felt discouraged like Grace in this story. When I told my parents what my brothers had said, they reminded me that I could do anything if I tried hard enough. Just like Grace's mom and Nana encouraged her, my mom and dad encouraged me. The next day, I went outside and played catch with my brothers and showed them that I could do it. Grace was determined to show others what she could do, and so was I.

Library Map Sample

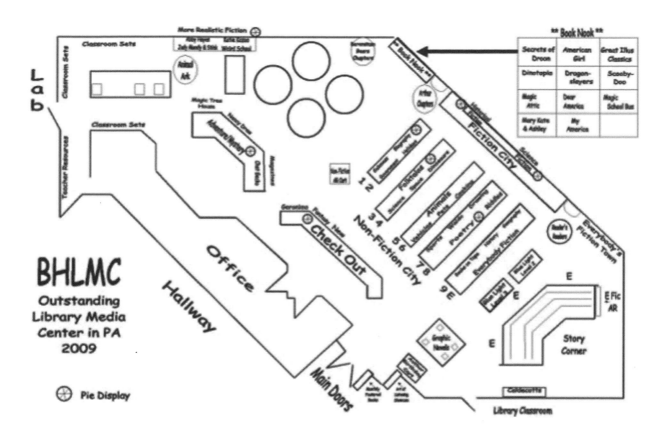

Book Talk Questions

1. Would you read another book by this author? Why or why not?

2. What was your favorite part of the book? Why?

3. If you could change any event in the story, what would it be and why?

4. Does the main character remind you of someone that you know? Why?

5. How did this story make you feel? Why?

6. Do you suppose the character would feel/act the same if . . . .

7. Can you list 3 things this character might need/want?

8. Is there a conversation in this book that you remember? Why?

9. I wonder why . . . .

10. I think . . . .

11. I was surprised when . . .

12. I didn't like it when . . .

13. Imagine that you're a friend of _____, how would you react if . . .

14. Was there a part of this story that you didn't understand?

15. Can you invent a new title for this book?

Million Dollar Words to Use for Book Discussions

adventurous	gentle	artistic	athletic
respectful	active	humble	brave
sloppy	bold	honest	serious
intelligent	successful	cheerful	independent
curious	inventive	creative	courageous
considerate	messy	selfish	daring
mischievous	neat	exciting	warm
trustworthy	proud	open	wild
dangerous	entertaining	embarrassed	shy
dainty	studious	lazy	bossy
hostile	generous	witty	friendly
nervous	curious	scared	confident
worried	angry	intimidated	humorous

 From *Personalized Reading: It's a Piece of PIE* by Nancy Hobbs, Kristen Sacco, and Myra R. Oleynik. Santa Barbara, CA: Libraries Unlimited. Copyright © 2011.

PIE Parent Letter

Dear Parents,

As part of a comprehensive language arts program, our class will be participating in a year-long reading project called PIE. Below you will find a description of the program. Your child has been asked to take their PIE folder home this weekend to show you and tell you about what they have learned. Students will have some time to read in class, but will also need to read at home. We will be working closely with our school librarian, as we read and write about the different reading genres. Please let me know if you have any questions about this program. The students are excited to start this process, and are looking forward to sharing their progress with you this year.

What is PIE?
A Personalized, Independent Enrichment program for reading

PIE is a personalized, independent, enrichment program for readers of all abilities. Students choose books from 8 different genres displayed on a PIE chart. The genres include: realistic fiction, fantasy, biography, historical fiction, adventure/mystery, science fiction, poetry and nonfiction. The teacher and librarian introduce the individual genres through classroom lessons, read-alouds and book chats.

The book selection and order of the genres read is the student's choice, making the program personal. For each book read, students are asked to maintain a reading log to track their progress. Once the student has finished the book, he/she will complete a Story Element Summary (SES). Story Element Summaries provide a framework that highlights the characters, setting and plot of the story. Students meet in small groups with the teacher and or librarian on a weekly basis to share either their SES or the progress they have made on the book. After students share their SES, they write the title of the book and color that slice of the genre on their PIE chart. When all parts of the PIE are completed, the students will choose one of the books they've read and complete a project to extend their learning about that story. Once students share their project with their PIE group, the process begins again with the selection of a new book based on a genre from the next PIE chart.

The program is independent because the students move through PIE charts at their own pace. Students begin the year with a four-genre PIE chart that includes realistic fiction, fantasy, biography and historical fiction. After students have completed all of the steps for each book read, they are given a second PIE chart with four additional genres; science fiction, poetry, adventure/mystery, and nonfiction. Once this PIE chart is complete, an eight piece PIE chart which includes all of the genres is given to the student. Students can complete as many eight-piece PIE charts as possible throughout the school year.

When students have the opportunity to choose their own books, write about them, and talk about the stories with their classmates, they come to realize how books can enrich their lives.

Thank you,

From *Personalized Reading: It's a Piece of PIE* by Nancy Hobbs, Kristen Sacco, and Myra R. Oleynik. Santa Barbara, CA: Libraries Unlimited. Copyright © 2011.

Lesson 1: Introduction to the PIE Program

AASL Standards: 1.1.2, 1.1.3, 1.1.9, and 2.1.2

Objectives: SWBAT

1. Understand the purpose of the PIE program.
2. Demonstrate how to use a reading log.
3. Understand the teacher's expectations for the program.

Materials: One for Each Student

1. Pocket folder
2. Reading log
3. Assignment sheet
4. First four-piece PIE sheet
5. Story element guide for fiction books
6. Composition notebook

Procedure

1. Ask the students to meet in front of the teacher.
2. Tell them that they are going to learn about a new independent reading program called PIE.
3. Tell the students that PIE is an independent reading program that will allow them to choose their own books at their own reading level.
4. Ask the students the following questions:
   - *What is one way to become a better reader?*
   - *Where do you go to find a book that you want to read?*
   - *When you want to find a good book to read, who do you go to see?*
   - *How do you know if the book you choose is right for you?*
   - *Where do you read?*
   - *What do you do when you don't like a book?*

- *Do you ever have the opportunity to talk about what you are reading with other students?*

- *Why is it important to talk about what we are reading?*

5. As students answer these questions, help them to formulate the following ideas: Students become good readers by

   - Reading independently

   - Reading books of interest

   - Writing about the books they read

   - Discussing the books they read with others.

6. Tell the students: *The program we are going to learn about is going to help us become "lifelong" readers. We will have the opportunity to read a book of choice, learn about the various types of books that are available to us, and talk about the books we are reading with our peers. One of the people that will help us to choose books that are right for us is Ms./Mr. _____ (the library media specialist.) He or she is a partner in this program and will help us to make informed decisions about books.*

7. Tell the students that they will each have a pocket folder that will become their PIE folder.

8. Pass out student PIE folders.

9. Go over each of the materials that are found in this folder.

10. Begin with the reading log. Tell the students that each time they choose a book from the library, they will fill out the information at the top of the page. As they read their books, they will write down the date that they read and the page numbers read. The purpose of the reading log is to keep track of student's reading. It will help the teacher to know how many pages are being read each time and how often a student is reading.

11. Tell the students to take out their PIE assignment sheet. Explain to the students: *Each week we will meet in a small group to check your progress with this program. During our PIE meeting, we will use the assignment sheet to track your progress. Each week before our PIE meeting, please refer back to this to make sure that you are staying on track.*

12. Ask the students if they know what the word *genre* means. Explain that a genre is a category that books are put into in the library. It helps to group literature.

13. Introduce the four-piece PIE. Explain: *We will be working with eight different genres this year. Throughout the next few months, you will learn more about each genre. The first four that you will be working with are realistic fiction, fantasy, biography, and historical fiction As you finish reading and writing about your books, you will color in the completed piece of PIE on this PIE sheet.*

14. Introduce the story element guide and composition book. Explain: *This guide will be used to write about what you are reading. We will focus on the story elements character,*

setting, and plot. All story element information will be written in your composition book. This will help us to look back at what we have read over the course of the year.

15. Close the lesson by referring back to the questions asked at the beginning of the lesson. Ask:

   • How do you think this program will help us to become better readers?

   • How do you think Mr./Ms. _____ (library media specialist) can help us make good book choices?

   • What are you most looking forward to when starting this program?

Lesson 2: Genre Overview Lesson

Teacher and Librarian Co-teach Lesson
Please note: This lesson may be taught in two sessions, depending on time restrictions.
AASL Standards: 1.1.2, 1.1.6, 3.2.3, 4.1.5

Objectives: SWBAT
1. Identify two elements of at least four featured genres from a list of 8 genres, including: realistic fiction, science fiction, historical fiction, fantasy fiction, poetry, biography, mystery/adventure fiction, and non-fiction/informational

Materials:
1. Different books on display
2. Numbers 1–8
3. Genre terms
4. Genre Detective Sheet First PIE and/or Second PIE

Procedure:
1. LW (Librarian will) + TW (Teacher will) build background for PIE in the library. "When you hear us talk about PIE, it means that we will be referring to Personalized Independent Enrichment. From now on, we want you to think of the library as a place for choices. Think of it as your favorite restaurant where you are allowed to order for yourself. No one is going to order for you. That's why it's personal. In a restaurant, foods are grouped on the menu such as appetizers, salads, and desserts which you always review before you place your order. Books are also organized in our library and in our classroom to make it simpler to locate them. But today we're not going to tell you what is on the menu here in the library. You're going to have to taste test the books yourself and describe what you think these books have in common."

2. LW label 8 display areas of books throughout the library with numbers 1–8. Divide the class into 8 groups and position them throughout with the purpose of determining why certain books have been grouped together in these displays. Students will be given a Genre Detective Sheet to fill in when they visit a display. Ask students the following

(continued)

questions: What do they notice about the books in their display? Look at the spines, what are some common elements? Jot down several examples of each. Teacher and librarian should visit the displays to listen in on student conversations.

3. After several minutes students will rotate groups to label the next display with their findings. After 3 rotations, gather students together to share their findings in front of a projector or Smartboard.

4. TW open a word processing document to create a word cloud. Ask students to provide their classifications and descriptions for each genre, which will serve as a sign to post above each genre display. These word clouds, also known as Wordles may be printed for the students to keep in their PIE notebooks. Visit www.wordle.net to learn more. Students may vote for their favorites to post in their classroom and in the library.

5. LW conclude by surveying students and asking which genre slice of PIE they plan to sink their teeth into first? You can also check for understanding using CPS clickers or create your questions on Quia.com.

Genre Detective

Be a Genre Detective

Clues: First PIE

events could happen	animals that talk	believable	**magic**
realistic characters	**fairies**	**impossible strategies**	**friends**	ordinary
make-believe	good vs evil	everyday life	**common problems**
supernatural powers	creatures	**normal**	**unusual setting**

Realistic Fiction

_____
_____
_____
_____
_____
_____

Fantasy Fiction

_____
_____
_____
_____
_____
_____

---

ordinary people	**historically accurate**	believable	**about a famous person**
old-fashioned clothing characters	all real events	fictional events	**realistic**
setting in the past	**time line**	index	**table of contents**	in the present day

---

Historical Fiction

_____
_____
_____
_____
_____
_____

Biography

_____
_____
_____
_____
_____
_____

Be a Genre Detective

Clues: Second PIE

events could happen	**unrealistic story elements**	**detectives**	**time travel**
hard to Believe	action **aliens**	**solutions** *clues*	conflict
realistic characters	**superhuman powers**	life in the future *robots*	adventures

Science Fiction

_____

_____

_____

_____

_____

_____

Adventure/ Mystery Fiction

_____

_____

_____

_____

_____

_____

photographs	emotions and feelings	*just the facts*	learn something new
rhyme	*diagrams*	not from imagination	table of contents **haiku**
alliteration	**rhythm**	plays with language	**table of contents** often funny

Poetry

_____

_____

_____

_____

_____

_____

Non-Fiction Informational

_____

_____

_____

_____

_____

_____

Lesson 3: Introduction to Elements of a Realistic Fiction Story

AASL Standards: 1.1.6, 2.1.2, 4.1.1, and 4.1.3

Objectives: SWBAT

1. Demonstrate understanding of realistic fiction elements.
2. Demonstrate understanding of story elements.

Materials: One for Each Student

1. Copy of *Amazing Grace* by Hoffman
2. Genre elements graphic organizer

Procedure

1. Tell the students that the story that you are going to read falls under the genre category of realistic fiction.
2. Read the story *Amazing Grace* by Hoffman to the students.
3. Tell the students: *As I read* Amazing Grace *to you, I want you to notice what about this story makes it a "realistic fiction?"*
4. Pass out genre elements graphic organizers, pencils, and clipboards to students. Ask them to come join you in a common area in your classroom.
5. Tell the students: *As I read, jot down ideas and clues you have about what makes this story realistic on your graphic organizer. Also remember to pay attention to the character, setting, and plot of the story.*
6. Read the story. Encourage the students to jot down ideas. As you read, pause and ask questions to help to point out realistic fiction clues.
7. After you finish reading the story, ask the students to answer the following questions:
   - *Who was the main character of the story?* (**character**)
   - *Where did the story take place?* (**setting**)
   - *What happened in the beginning, middle, and end of the story?* (**plot**)
8. Ask the students to share the clues they found in the story that make it a realistic fiction book. On an overhead or computer projector, the teacher writes ideas as the students share.
9. Ask the students to write ideas in their graphic organizers as the students share.
10. Close the lesson by reviewing elements found in realistic fiction stories.

Lesson 4: Introduction to Elements of a Fantasy Story

AASL Standards: 1.1.2, 2.1.2, 4.1.1, and 4.1.3

Objectives: SWBAT

1. Demonstrate understanding of fantasy elements.
2. Demonstrate understanding of story elements.

Materials

1. Copy of *Dear Mrs. Larue* by Teague
2. Genre elements graphic organizer

Procedure

1. Tell the students that the story that you are going to read falls under the genre category of fantasy.

2. Read the story *Dear Mrs. Larue* by Teague to the students.

3. Tell the students: *As I read* Dear Mrs. Larue *to you, I want you to notice what about this story makes it a "fantasy."*

4. Pass out genre elements graphic organizers, pencils, and clipboards to students. Ask them to come join you in a common area in your classroom.

5. Tell the students: *As I read, jot down ideas and clues you have about what makes this story a fantasy on your graphic organizer. Also remember to pay attention to the character, setting, and plot of the story.*

6. Read the story. Encourage the students to jot down ideas. As you read, pause and ask questions to help to point out fantasy clues.

7. After you finish reading the story, ask the students to answer the following questions:

   - *Who was the main character of the story?* (**character**)

   - *Where did the story take place?* (**setting**)

   - *What happened in the beginning, middle, and end of the story?* (**plot**)

8. Ask the students to share the clues they found in the story that makes it a fantasy. On an overhead or computer projector, the teacher writes ideas as the students share.

9. Ask the students to write ideas in their graphic organizers as the students share.

10. Close the lesson by reviewing elements found in fantasy stories.

Lesson 5: Compare and Contrast Elements of a Realistic Fiction and Fantasy Story

AASL Standards: 2.1.2, 3.2.3, 4.1.5, and 4.1.6

Objectives: SWBAT

1. Demonstrate understanding of realistic fiction elements.

2. Demonstrate understanding of fantasy elements.

3. Demonstrate understanding of story elements.

Materials

1. Copy of *Amazing Grace* by Hoffman

2. Copy of *Dear Mrs. Larue* by Teague

3. Genre elements graphic organizer completed in two previous lessons

4. Genre comparison sheet

Procedure

1. Ask the students to meet you in a common area of the classroom. Explain: *Our last two PIE lessons focused on the genres of realistic fiction and fantasy. Today we are going to compare and contrast the elements of each genre. I want you to think about what is similar and different about the two stories that we read,* Amazing Grace *and* Dear Mrs. Larue. *Work with a partner to complete the genre comparison sheet.*

2. Group the students and ask them to complete the genre comparison sheet together.

3. Give the students a reasonable amount of time to complete the graphic organizer and then ask them to meet with you.

4. Discuss their ideas as you add the ideas to an overhead or projection of the genre comparison sheet.

5. Highlight the idea that although realistic fiction and fantasy are very different in many ways, because they are both fictional, they contain characters, settings, and a plot. Stressing this idea with students will help them better understand the parts of the story element guide introduced in the next lesson.

6. Close the lesson by reviewing information that students generated about this topic.

Lesson 6: How to Write a Summary

AASL Standards: 1.3.1, 3.1.3, and 4.1.3

Objectives: SWBAT

1. Demonstrate understanding of how to write a summary.

Materials

1. Chart paper with names of fairy tales written at the top along with a story starter.
2. Markers
3. Copies of favorite fairy tales the students have previously read

Procedure

1. Ask the students to come to a common area in the classroom.

2. Explain: *Today we are going to learn how to write a summary. What is a summary? How long should a summary be? What parts should you include in your summary?*

3. As students respond help them to understand the importance of including only the big ideas of the story, being sure to include events from the beginning, middle, and end of the story.

4. Explain: *We are going to have a "summary relay." I am going to place you into groups of five. Your group's job is to write five sentences summarizing one of these popular fairy tales that we all have heard many times throughout our lives. (Refer to copies of the fairy tales.) Your group will line up in front of one of the pieces of chart paper that you see displayed around the room. Each person is responsible for adding one sentence to the group summary. When you are finished writing your sentence, go to the back of the line and sit down to show that you are finished. Make sure that before adding your sentence, you read the sentence that comes before your sentence. Also, make sure that the sentence you add tells the big ideas of the story and continues the sequential order of the story. Each group will have 10 minutes to write the summary. This is* not *a race to see who finishes first. The time limit is just to help you to stay focused on the activity and to make sure you do not spend too much time on one sentence.*

5. Group the students and send them to one of the five chart papers displayed throughout the classroom.

6. Set the timer for 10 minutes and tell the students to begin.

7. Ask each group to complete a self-evaluation of their work using the self-evaluation rubric. Tell them to give themselves one point for each part included in their summary.

8. When time is up, bring the class together and share their summaries and self-evaluations.

9. Discuss with the students the things that made this activity difficult and how it forced them to stick with the most important ideas.

10. Close the lesson by listing the characteristics of a summary.

Lesson 7: How to Write a Connection

AASL Standards: 4.1.1, 4.1.3, and 4.1.5

Objectives: SWBAT

1. Understand the different types of connections.

2. Find various types of connections within their reading.

Materials

1. Chart paper labeled with each type of connection; text-to-self (TS), text-to-text (TT), or text-to-world (TW).

2. Each poster should have a connection written at the top as an example.

3. Post-It notes

4. A recording of the story *Alexander and the Terrible, Horrible, No Good, Very Bad Day* by Judith Viorst

Procedure

1. Hang chart paper with the following connection headings in three different parts of the room.

   • Text-to-self (TS)

   • Text-to-text (TT)

   • Text-to-world (TW)

2. Select a story in which students are familiar to demonstrate an example for each type of connection. This could include a recent novel, read-aloud, or basal story. These connections will be written at the top of each chart paper.

3. Pass out Post-It notes to each student.

4. Tell them that they will be asked to listen to the book *Alexander and the Terrible, Horrible, No Good, Very Bad Day* by Judith Viorst and find one connection to the story. They can choose any one of the three types.

5. Students listen to the story and write their connection on a Post-It note.

6. After finished, ask the students to stick their Post-Its to the corresponding chart paper. (All of the students with a text-to-self connection will stick their Post-It on the chart paper labeled "text-to-self," and so on.)

7. After the Post-Its have been placed, call the students back to the carpet and choose a few examples to share.

8. As examples are shared, brainstorm a list of ways to write a quality connection.

9. Ask the students to point out connections that include the characteristics found on the tip sheet.

10. Close the lesson by discussing the following question:

    • *How does making connections with the books we read help to improve our comprehension of the story?*

11. Through this discussion, help students to surmise that as we develop quality connections with the stories we read, we begin to understand the story at a deeper level, which helps to build our knowledge of the story.

Lesson 8: Introduction to How to Write a Story Element Summary

AASL Standards: 1.1.6, 1.3.4, 2.1.5, and 2.4.3

Objectives: SWBAT

1. Demonstrate understanding of character, setting, and plot.

2. Understand how to write a connection to a book they have read.

3. Use the elements of a story to create a summary by putting the plot in sequential order.

Materials

1. Overhead or projection of story element guide

2. Poster board for a small group of students

3. Glue

4. Scissors

5. Markers

6. One copy per group of the story elements from *Dear Mrs. Larue* by Teague

Procedure

1. Project the story element guide and highlight the parts that are included.

2. Discuss the events of the book *Dear Mrs. Larue* by Teague read during a previous lesson.

3. Break the students into small groups. Explain: *Each group will be given a series of sentences that relate to the story* Dear Mrs. Larue. *Follow the story element guide and label each of the story elements and connections in the correct order. Work together to create a story element sheet by using these sentences and gluing them onto the poster board.*

4. Tell the students to get their materials and go to their group work area.

5. Allow a reasonable amount of time for students to complete the assignment.

6. After the groups have completed the task, share the finished product.

7. Close the lesson by turning off the projection of the story element guide and asking students to see if they can remember the parts of the story element guide in sequential order.

Lesson 9: How to Write a Fiction Story Element Summary

AASL Standards: 1.1.2, 2.1.2, 2.1.3, and 3.1.3

Objectives: SWBAT

1. Demonstrate understanding of character, setting, and plot.
2. Understand how to write a connection to a book read previously read.
3. Write a summary.

Materials

1. Student copy of the fiction story element guide
2. Blank composition paper
3. A copy of a book or story read previously by the students in the classroom.

Procedure

1. Explain: *Today each of you will have the opportunity to write your own story element summary. Remember the story _____ that we read _____.*
2. Discuss.
3. Display the story element guide on overhead projector or projection machine.
4. At this point, each of the categories should be familiar to the students. Review each element and show students how to set up their paper.
5. See the story element summary sample
6. Remind students of the importance of including each of the category titles such as **Genre** or **Characters** on their paper to make sure that their story element summary is organized properly. It may take some students longer to master this, so continue to reteach as necessary.
7. Review how to write a quality connection to a story they've read.
8. Pair students or ask the students to complete independently a Story Element Summary for the book read previously in the classroom.
9. While the students are working, monitor progress and work with students as necessary. It is well worth the time it takes to teach this process correctly.
10. To close the lesson, ask the students to share their story element summaries in small groups.

Lesson 10: How to Write a Biography Story Element Summary

AASL Standards: 1.1.4, 2.1.2, 2.1.3, 2.4.1, and 4.1.6

Objectives: SWBAT

1. Demonstrate understanding of a person's life events.

2. Understand how to write a connection to a biography.

3. Compare and contrast fiction with nonfiction biography.

Materials

1. Genre comparison sheet for biography (nonfiction) versus fiction

2. Overhead of genre comparison sheet

3. A biography of choice

4. Student copy of biography story element guide

5. Blank composition paper

Procedure

Before completing this lesson, it may be helpful to schedule a biography book talk with your librarian.

1. Explain: *We have learned how to write a story element summary based on a fictional story. Today we will learn how to write one after reading a biography. As I read this biography, I want you to notice the differences between a fictional story and a biography, which is nonfiction.*

2. Read the biography.

3. Ask the students to work with a partner to tell similarities and differences of fiction versus nonfiction biography on their genre comparison sheet.

4. Pull the students back together as a group.

5. As the students share information, write their responses on the genre comparison sheet overhead or projection.

6. Discuss the similarities and differences.

7. Display the biography story element guide on an overhead projector or projection machine.

8. Discuss categories and ask the students to notice the differences and similarities to a Fiction Story Element Guide.

9. Remind students of the importance of including each of the category titles such as: **Characters** or **Life Events** on their paper to make sure that their biography story element summary is organized properly.

10. On the overhead or projection, create a biography story element summary together as a group for the biography you have just read.

11. To close lesson, ask the students to review the parts of a biography story element guide and where they can be found in the classroom when students are ready to use them.

Lesson 11: How to Create a Project After Completing a PIE

AASL Standards: 1.3.5, 3.1.3, 4.1.3, and 4.1.5

Objectives: SWBAT

1. Demonstrate understanding a story.
2. Use creative expression to tell about a story read.

Materials

1. Project ideas
2. Samples of completed PIE projects, if available

Procedure

1. Explain: *After you have finished reading each of the four genres on the first PIE chart, you will be asked to complete a small project about one of the four books that you read. The purpose of the project is to deepen your comprehension of the story, allow you an opportunity to use your creativity to share information about the book, and help your PIE group develop a better understanding of the story.*

2. Explain: *The first thing that you will do is choose a project to complete.* **Please see the project ideas.** *After you have decided on a project, decide which of the four books you would like to tell more about.*

3. Tell the students that they need to write a rough draft of the project, edit, and then publish the project in some way so that it can be displayed in the classroom or the library.

4. It is important that students understand that this project is not meant to be elaborate; however, it should be neat work that others would be interested in viewing.

5. Share examples of previous projects if available.

6. To close the lesson, ask the students to brainstorm ideas of how to publish their work.

7. Post these ideas in the classroom for students to view when they are ready to create a PIE project.

Lesson 12: How to Write a Poetry Story Element Summary

AASL Standards: 2.1.2, 3.1.2, 3.1.3, and 4.1.5

Objectives: SWBAT

1. Demonstrate understanding of a how poems are written.

2. Understand how to write a connection to a poem.

Materials

1. A poetry book of choice

2. Student copy of the poetry story element guide

3. Blank transparency, one for each pair of students

4. Transparency markers, one for each pair of students

Procedure

Before completing this lesson, it may be helpful to schedule a poetry book talk with your librarian.

1. Explain: *We have learned how to write a story element summary based on a fictional story and how to write one based on a biography. Today we will learn how to write for poetry. As I read these poems, I want you to notice the differences between a fictional story and a poetry book.*

2. Read the poetry book.

3. Discuss the similarities and differences.

4. To each set of partners, pass out a copy of a poem, a blank transparency, and a transparency marker.

5. Ask the students to use their blank transparencics to list the characters and setting of the poem.

6. Tell them to write a short paragraph telling what the poem is about and if there is a message to the poem.

7. Ask the students to write a connection to the poem. Remind them that they may write a text-to-text, text-to-self, or text-to-world connection.

8. After students have completed this, ask pairs of students to share their information by displaying their transparencies on the overhead projector.

From *Personalized Reading: It's a Piece of PIE* by Nancy Hobbs, Kristen Sacco, and Myra R. Oleynik. Santa Barbara, CA: Libraries Unlimited. Copyright © 2011.

9. As students display their information, highlight quality descriptions and connections.

10. Display the poetry story element guide on overhead projector.

11. Discuss the categories and ask the students to notice the differences and similarities to a fiction story element guide.

12. Make sure students understand that they do not need to write the poem on their story element summary; they only need to have the book handy when sharing with their PIE group.

13. Be sure to focus students' attention on the fact that they are required to choose two poems to share.

14. Remind students of the importance of including each of the category titles on their paper to make sure that their poetry story element summary is organized properly.

15. To close the lesson, ask the students to review the parts of a poetry story element guide and where they can be found in the classroom when students are ready to use them.

Lesson 13: How to Create a Nonfiction Informational Presentation

AASL Standards: 2.1.2, 3.1.3, 3.2.3, and 4.1.5

Objectives: SWBAT

1. Demonstrate understanding a nonfiction topic
2. Use creative expression to tell about information learned

Materials

1. Nonfiction informational presentation guide
2. Nonfiction informational book
3. Nonfiction graphic organizer
4. Ideas for a quality presentation sheet

Procedure

Before completing this lesson, it may be helpful to schedule a nonfiction informational book talk with your librarian.

1. Explain: *We have learned how to write story element summaries for fiction, biography, and poetry. Today we will learn how to create a presentation for a nonfiction informational selection with the use of the nonfiction informational presentation guide. As I read this book, jot down facts that you have learned about the subject on your nonfiction graphic organizer.*

2. Read a nonfiction book of choice.

3. After the book has been read and the students have written down their ideas, split them into small groups.

4. Pass out the ideas for a quality presentation sheet to groups.

5. Ask the students to work as a group to brainstorm creative but possible ways to present the information they learned.

6. Allow the students approximately 10 minutes to brainstorm ideas.

7. Bring the groups together and list ideas that were generated.

8. Tell the students that you will make a list of the ideas generated from the class for them to keep in their PIE folders along with the nonfiction informational presentation guide.

9. Share the presentation guide with students on the overhead projector. Discuss how this is a guide for them to prepare their presentation and the differences between it and the other guide sheets.

10. Close the lesson by explaining to students that this is an opportunity to show what they know and have learned about a particular subject and are permitted to use creative ways to do so.

11. Teacher's note: We usually have students share their presentations with the entire class rather than just their PIE group.

Historical Fiction Book Chat

AASL Standards:

1.1.2

1.1.3

1.1.6

1.2.2

2.4.4

Objectives: SWBAT

1. Define the elements of historical fiction.

2. Formulate opinions about historical fiction titles.

Materials: Star Review Sheets, Crayons, Clipboards

Procedure:
TW Schedule at least 40 minutes for an Historical Fiction Book Chat with the librarian. Discuss background on recent class activities.

LW Gather materials several days prior to the class visit to ensure availability. Gather background on featured authors, a relevant website, props, and any personal connections that you might be able to make to these titles. Read the books you plan to share ahead of time or at least have enough knowledge to "chat" and "tease" rather than to "read" and "report" about each. It is also possible to paraphrase from the jacket flaps or affix sticky notes for talking points on the backs of each. Begin with a catchy first line or quote to add interest and build suspense.

Plan your transitions from title to title purposefully to be sure to find connections between characters, themes, time periods, and settings. This will allow your book talk to flow. Having props such as an old letter, an antique, old money, or a piece of vintage clothing will also help to redirect students' attention.

TW Build excitement in the classroom by reading aloud an historical fiction picture book and announcing that more books like this one will be awaiting them in the library. Make connections with the students on background that they may have experienced, "How many of you have taken a vacation to Williamsburg, Plymouth, etc. and provide time to discuss and encourage children to bring in souvenirs or related vacation photos.

LW Seat students with their PIE folders in a comfortable corner of the library. Distribute clipboards with Star Reviews and crayons. Explain the Star Review as a way for students to express their personal opinions about the books they will hear about today. This is similar to how adults review movies and restaurants. Teacher and Librarian should interject throughout the book chat to add their own personal impressions and experiences.

TW Recall what was discussed in classroom conversation regarding historical fiction.

LW Build background on the Historical Fiction genre emphasizing that before an author writes an historical fiction book he or she must carefully research their topic. See Appendix. Projecting the Magic Treehouse Time Slider http://www.randomhouse.com/kids/magictreehouse/timeslider.html or using Scholastic's Interactive Timeline http://teacher.scholastic.com/activities/our_america/index_noflash.htm will help students to gain an understanding of various settings in history. American Girl books also have a wonderful section in the back of each where photographs, illustrations, and informational text offer a Peek into the Past.

TW Set a purpose for listening with students

LW Share titles while referring to the student Star Reviews and pointing out the author's last name and how it corresponds to the call letters on the spines of each book. Remind students to fill in their designated amount of stars after listening to the descriptions of each.

TW Direct students to rank their top 3 choices heard during the Book Chat on their Star Review for next time. They should also plan where their first steps will take them by asking themselves questions such as, "What is the last name of my author?" "I'd like to read about others by that same author on the OPAC."

LW + TW Provide time for students to browse through the library to select these or other historical fiction books reminding them to read the spines, use the library OPAC, read book teasers, and to ask questions of each other. Keeping this Star Review in their PIE folder will also provide students with a resource when they return to the library along with their library maps and scavenger hunt photos.

Tech Link—As a follow-up the librarian may want to preserve the essence of this historical fiction book chat by recording it as a podcast and posting to the library webpage, blog or wiki. Students may also be encouraged to listen to Nancy Kean's daily book podcasts at http://nancykeane.com/rss.html.

92 OBA	Barack Obama	☆☆☆
92 CLE	Roberto Clemente Baseball Legend	☆☆☆
92 DEP	* 26 Fairmont Avenue	☆☆☆
92 GAN	Gandhi	☆☆☆
92 KEN	John F. Kennedy, The Making of a Leader	☆☆☆
92 PAT	Danica Patrick	☆☆☆
92 PIC	Picasso	☆☆☆
92 SIL	Shel Silverstein	☆☆☆
92 SIT	Sitting Bull	☆☆☆
92 SOS	At the Plate with Sammy Sosa	☆☆☆
92 SPI	Steven Spielberg	☆☆☆
92 KEL	Who Was Helen Keller?	☆☆☆

92 OBA	Wheeler, Jill	Barack Obama	☆☆☆

92 OBA	Wheeler, Jill	Barack Obama	☆☆☆
92 CLE	Healy, Nick	Roberto Clemente Baseball Legend	☆☆☆
92 DEP	DePaola, Tomie	* 26 Fairmont Avenue	☆☆☆
92 GAN	Demi	Gandhi	☆☆☆
92 KEN	Time For Kids, Upadhyay, Ritu	John F. Kennedy, The Making of a Leader	☆☆☆
92 PAT	Glaser, Jason	Danica Patrick	☆☆☆
92 PIC	Venezia, Mike	Picasso	☆☆☆
92 SIL	Meister, Cari	Shel Silverstein	☆☆☆
92 SIT	Trumbauer, Lisa	Sitting Bull	☆☆☆
92 SOS	Christopher, Matt	At the Plate with Sammy Sosa	☆☆☆
92 SPI	Brown, Jonathan	Steven Spielberg	☆☆☆
92 KEL	Thompson, Gare	Who Was Helen Keller?	☆☆☆

92 OBA	Wheeler, Jill	Barack Obama	☆☆☆
92 CLE	Healy, Nick	Roberto Clemente Baseball Legend	☆☆☆
92 DEP	DePaola Tomie	* 26 Fairmont Avenue	☆☆☆
92 GAN	Demi	Gandhi	☆☆☆
92 KEN	Time For Kids, Upadhyay, Ritu	John F. Kennedy, The Making of a Leader	☆☆☆
92 PAT	Glaser, Jason	Danica Patrick	☆☆☆
92 PIC	Venezia, Mike	Picasso	☆☆☆
92 SIL	Meister, Cari	Shel Silverstein	☆☆☆
92 SIT	Trumbauer, Lisa	Sitting Bull	☆☆☆
92 SOS	Christopher, Matt	At the Plate with Sammy Sosa	☆☆☆
92 SPI	Brown, Jonatha	Steven Spielberg	☆☆☆
92 KEL	Thompson, Gare	Who Was Helen Keller?	☆☆☆

Biography Star Review Sheet

"Students may use the following key to indicate their level of enthusiasm for each book.

☆☆ I probably won't check out this book.

★★ I might check out this book.

★★★ I definitely want to check out this book!

From *Personalized Reading: It's a Piece of PIE* by Nancy Hobbs, Kristen Sacco, and Myra R. Oleynik. Santa Barbara, CA: Libraries Unlimited. Copyright © 2011.

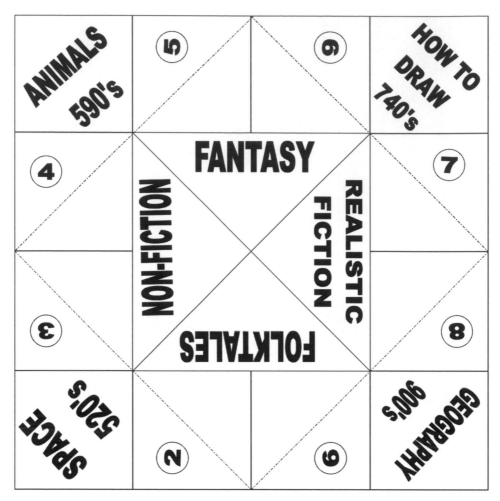

Having trouble deciding what to read? Make a "Cootie-Catcher/Fortune Teller" for fun!

FIC ASC	Asch, Frank	Class Pets, The Ghost of P.S. 42	☆☆☆
FIC AVI	Avi	Poppy	☆☆☆
FIC DAH	Dahl, Roald	The Twits	☆☆☆
FIC HOR	Horvath, Polly	The Trolls	☆☆☆
FIC JON	Jones, Marcia Thornton	Ghostville Elementary, New Ghoul in School	☆☆☆
FIC KIN	King-Smith, Dick	Harriet's Hare	☆☆☆
FIC KOL	Koller, Jackie French	Dragons of Krad	☆☆☆
FIC MAR	Martin, Ann	The Meanest Doll in the World	☆☆☆
FIC MEA	Meadows, Daisy	Rainbow Magic Fairies Georgia the Guinea Pig Fairy	☆☆☆
FIC PET	Peterson, John	The Littles	☆☆☆
FIC STI	Stilton, Geronimo	The Phantom of the Subway	☆☆☆
FIC WHI	White, E.B.	Charlotte's Web	☆☆☆

FIC ASC	Asch, Frank	Class Pets, The Ghost of P.S. 42	☆☆☆
FIC AVI	Avi	Poppy	☆☆☆
FIC DAH	Dahl, Roald	The Twits	☆☆☆
FIC HOR	Horvath, Polly	The Trolls	☆☆☆
FIC JON	Jones, Marcia Thornton	Ghostville Elementary, New Ghoul in School	☆☆☆
FIC KIN	King-Smith, Dick	Harriet's Hare	☆☆☆
FIC KOL	Koller, Jackie French	Dragons of Krad	☆☆☆
FIC MAR	Martin, Ann	The Meanest Doll in the World	☆☆☆
FIC MEA	Meadows, Daisy	Rainbow Magic Fairies Georgia the Guinea Pig Fairy	☆☆☆
FIC PET	Peterson, John	The Littles	☆☆☆
FIC STI	Stilton, Geronimo	The Phantom of the Subway	☆☆☆
FIC WHI	White, E.B.	Charlotte's Web	☆☆☆

Fantasy Star Review Sheet

"Students may use the following key to indicate their level of enthusiasm for each book.

☆☆☆ I probably won't check out this book.

★★☆ I might check out this book.

★★★ I definitely want to check out this book!

Call #	Author	Series / Title	Rating
FIC ABB	Abbott, Tony	Secrets of Droon series	☆☆☆
FIC BRO	Brown, Jeff	Flat Stanley series	☆☆☆
FIC CHR	Christian, Peggy	The Bookstore Mouse	☆☆☆
FIC COV	Coville, Bruce	Moongobble and Me series and The Monster's Ring	☆☆☆
FIC DET	DeTerlizzi, Tony	Spiderwick series	☆☆☆
FIC DUE	Duey, Kathleen	The Unicorn's Secret series	☆☆☆
FIC GAN	Gannett, Ruth	My Father's Dragon series	☆☆☆
FIC HUR	Hurwitz, Johanna	Pee Wee & Plush	☆☆☆
FIC LeG	LeGuin, Ursula K.	Catwings series	☆☆☆
FIC LEV	Levine, Gail Carson	Fairy Dust and the Quest for the Egg	☆☆☆
FIC MAC MUL	McMullan, Kate	Dragon Slayers' Academy	☆☆☆
FIC STR	Strauss, Linda Leopold	A Fairy Called Hilary	☆☆☆

Fantasy Series Star Review Sheet

"Students may use the following key to indicate their level of enthusiasm for each book.

☆ I probably won't check out this book.

☆ I might check out this book.

★ I definitely want to check out this book!

Call #	Author	Series / Title	Rating
FIC ABB	Abbott, Tony	Secrets of Droon series	☆☆☆
FIC BRO	Brown, Jeff	Flat Stanley series	☆☆☆
FIC CHR	Christian, Peggy	The Bookstore Mouse	☆☆☆
FIC COV	Coville, Bruce	Moongobble and Me series and The Monster's Ring	☆☆☆
FIC DET	DeTerlizzi, Tony	Spiderwick series	☆☆☆
FIC DUE	Duey, Kathleen	The Unicorn's Secret series	☆☆☆
FIC GAN	Gannett, Ruth	My Father's Dragon series	☆☆☆
FIC HUR	Hurwitz, Johanna	Pee Wee & Plush	☆☆☆
FIC LeG	LeGuin, Ursula K.	Catwings series	☆☆☆
FIC LEV	Levine, Gail Carson	Fairy Dust and the Quest for the Egg	☆☆☆
FIC MAC MUL	McMullan, Kate	Dragon Slayers' Academy	☆☆☆
FIC STR	Strauss, Linda Leopold	A Fairy Called Hilary	☆☆☆

Call No.	Author	Title	Rating
398.2 ERN	Ernst, Lisa	The Three Spinning Fairies	☆☆☆
398.2 JOH	Johnson, Paul	Jack Outwits the Giants	☆☆☆
398.2 KIM	Kimmel, Eric	Anansi and the Moss-Covered Rock	☆☆☆
398.2 KNU	Knutson, Barbara	Love and Roast Chicken	☆☆☆
398.2 PAT	Paterson, Katherine	The King's Equal	☆☆☆
398.2 SAN	San Souci, Robert	Young Arthur	☆☆☆
398.2 SAN	San Souci, Robert	The Talking Eggs	☆☆☆
398.2 STE	Steptoe, John	Mufaro's Beautiful Daughters	☆☆☆
398.2 STE	Stevens, Janet	Tops & Bottoms	☆☆☆
398.2 YOU	Young, Ed	Cat and Rat	☆☆☆
398.21 AYL	Aylesworth, Jim	The Gingerbread Man	☆☆☆
398.22 ROS	Rosales, Melodye	Leola and the Honeybears	☆☆☆

Folktale Star Review Sheet

"Students may use the following key to indicate their level of enthusiasm for each book.

☆☆☆ I probably won't check out this book.

☆★★ I might check out this book.

★★★ I definitely want to check out this book!

From *Personalized Reading: It's a Piece of PIE* by Nancy Hobbs, Kristen Sacco, and Myra R. Oleynik. Santa Barbara, CA: Libraries Unlimited. Copyright © 2011.

Call #	Author	Title	Rating
FIC	(Book Nook)	My America Series	☆☆☆
FIC	(Book Nook)	American Girl Series	☆☆☆
FIC ACK	Ackerman, Karen	The Night Crossing	☆☆☆
FIC BRA	Bradley, Kimberly	Ruthie's Gift	☆☆☆
FIC DAL	Dalgliesh, Alice	The Bears on Hemlock Mountain	☆☆☆
FIC DAL	Dalgliesh, Alice	The Courage of Sarah Noble	☆☆☆
FIC DEC	DeClements, Barthe	The Bite of the Gold Bug	☆☆☆
FIC KIN	Kinsey-Warnock, Natalie	Lumber Camp Library	☆☆☆
FIC ROO	Roop, Peter and Connie	Grace's Letter to Lincoln	☆☆☆
FIC WAD	Waddell, Martin	Little Obie and the Flood	☆☆☆
FIC WIL	Wilder, Laura Ingalls	Little House Series	☆☆☆

Historical Fiction Star Review Sheet

"Students may use the following key to indicate their level of enthusiasm for each book.

☆ I probably won't check out this book.

☆ I might check out this book.

★ I definitely want to check out this book!

From *Personalized Reading: It's a Piece of PIE* by Nancy Hobbs, Kristen Sacco, and Myra R. Oleynik. Santa Barbara, CA: Libraries Unlimited. Copyright © 2011.

Call No.	Author	Title	Rating
363.34 OSB	Osborne, Mary Pope	Tsunamis and Other Natural Disasters	☆☆☆
363.12 DUB	Dubowski, Mark	Titanic – The Disaster That Shocked The World	☆☆☆
523.48 LAN	Landau, Elaine	Pluto From Planet to Dwarf	☆☆☆
578.77 COL	Coldiron, Deborah	Coral	☆☆☆
595.4 GER	Gerholdt, James	Tarantula Spiders	☆☆☆
598.47 HOL	Holmes, Kevin	Penguins	☆☆☆
598.5 WHI	Whitehouse, Patricia	Ostrich	☆☆☆
599.4 BLA	Bland, Celia	Bats	☆☆☆
589.47 OSB	Osborne, Mary Pope	Penguins and Antarctica	☆☆☆
629.4 WIL	Wilkinson, Philip	Spacebusters – The Race To The Moon	☆☆☆
636.1 GEN	Gentle, Victor & Perry, Janet	Quarter Horses	☆☆☆
796.332 STE	Stewart, Mark	The New England Patriots	☆☆☆

Call No.	Author	Title	Rating
363.34 OSB	Osborne, Mary Pope	Tsunamis and Other Natural Disasters	☆☆☆
363.12 DUB	Dubowski, Mark	Titanic – The Disaster That Shocked The World	☆☆☆
523.48 LAN	Landau, Elaine	Pluto From Planet to Dwarf	☆☆☆
578.77 COL	Coldiron, Deborah	Coral	☆☆☆
595.4 GER	Gerholdt, James	Tarantula Spiders	☆☆☆
598.47 HOL	Holmes, Kevin	Penguins	☆☆☆
598.5 WHI	Whitehouse, Patricia	Ostrich	☆☆☆
599.4 BLA	Bland, Celia	Bats	☆☆☆
589.47 OSB	Osborne, Mary Pope	Penguins and Antarctica	☆☆☆
629.4 WIL	Wilkinson, Philip	Spacebusters – The Race To The Moon	☆☆☆
636.1 GEN	Gentle, Victor & Perry, Janet	Quarter Horses	☆☆☆
796.332 STE	Stewart, Mark	The New England Patriots	☆☆☆

Non-Fiction Informational Star Review Sheet

"Students may use the following key to indicate their level of enthusiasm for each book.

☆☆ I probably won't check out this book.

★★ I might check out this book.

★★★ I definitely want to check out this book!

Call No.	Author	Title	Rating
FIC BLU	Blume, Judy	Soupy Saturdays with the Pain & the Great One	☆☆☆
FIC CHI	Child, Lauren	Clarice Bean Spells Trouble	☆☆☆
FIC HAR	Harper, Charise	Just Grace	☆☆☆
FIC KLE	Klein, Abby	Ready, Freddy! Homework Hassles	☆☆☆
FIC LOV	Lovelace, Maud	Betsy and Tacy Go Downtown	☆☆☆
FIC LOW	Lowry, Lois	Gooney Bird Greene	☆☆☆
FIC MAC DON	McDonald, Megan	Judy Moody	☆☆☆
FIC MAR	Martin, Ann	The Kids in Ms. Colman's Class	☆☆☆
FIC MAZ	Mazer, Anne	Look Before You Leap!	☆☆☆
FIC MAZ	Mazer, Anne	Two Heads Are Better Than One	☆☆☆
FIC PEN	Pennypacker, Sara	The Talented Clementine	☆☆☆

Realistic Fiction Series Star Review Sheet

"Students may use the following key to indicate their level of enthusiasm for each book.

☆ I probably won't check out this book.

☆☆ I might check out this book.

★★★ I definitely want to check out this book!

From *Personalized Reading: It's a Piece of PIE* by Nancy Hobbs, Kristen Sacco, and Myra R. Oleynik. Santa Barbara, CA: Libraries Unlimited. Copyright © 2011.

Call #	Author	Title	Rating
FIC BLU	Blume, Judy	Superfudge	☆☆☆
FIC CAM	Cameron, Ann	More Stories Julian Tells	☆☆☆
FIC CHR	Christopher, Matt	Face Off	☆☆☆
FIC CLE	Clements, Andrew	Jake Drake Class Clown	☆☆☆
FIC DAN	Danziger, Paula	You Can't Eat Your Chicken Pox, Amber Brown	☆☆☆
FIC GIF	Giff, Patricia	Look Out, Washington, D.C.!	☆☆☆
FIC HUR	Hurwitz, Johanna	Oh No, Noah!	☆☆☆
FIC KER	Kerrin, Joseph	Martin Bridge Ready for Takeoff	☆☆☆
FIC KLI	Kline, Suzy	Horrible Harry Moves Up To Third Grade	☆☆☆
FIC MAR	Martin, Ann	Karen's School Bus	☆☆☆
FIC MAC	McDonald, Megan	Stink and the Incredible Super-Galactic Jawbreaker	☆☆☆
FIC RYL	Rylant, Cynthia	In Aunt Lucy's Kitchen	☆☆☆

Call #	Author	Title	Rating
FIC BLU	Blume, Judy	Superfudge	☆☆☆
FIC CAM	Cameron, Ann	More Stories Julian Tells	☆☆☆
FIC CHR	Christopher, Matt	Face Off	☆☆☆
FIC CLE	Clements, Andrew	Jake Drake Class Clown	☆☆☆
FIC DAN	Danziger, Paula	You Can't Eat Your Chicken Pox, Amber Brown	☆☆☆
FIC GIF	Giff, Patricia	Look Out, Washington, D.C.!	☆☆☆
FIC HUR	Hurwitz, Johanna	Oh No, Noah!	☆☆☆
FIC KER	Kerrin, Joseph	Martin Bridge Ready for Takeoff	☆☆☆
FIC KLI	Kline, Suzy	Horrible Harry Moves Up To Third Grade	☆☆☆
FIC MAR	Martin, Ann	Karen's School Bus	☆☆☆
FIC MAC	McDonald, Megan	Stink and the Incredible Super-Galactic Jawbreaker	☆☆☆
FIC RYL	Rylant, Cynthia	In Aunt Lucy's Kitchen	☆☆☆

Realistic Fiction Star Review Sheet

"Students may use the following key to indicate their level of enthusiasm for each book.

☆☆ I probably won't check out this book.

☆★ I might check out this book.

★★ I definitely want to check out this book!

Call#	Author	Realistic Fiction Characters	Realistic Fiction Characters
FIC BAG	Baglio, Ben	Animal Ark	☆☆☆
FIC BLU	Blume, Judy	Fudge, Pain, Great One	☆☆☆
FIC CAM	Cameron, Ann	Huey, Julian	☆☆☆
FIC CHI	Child, Lauren	Clarice Bean	☆☆☆
FIC CHR	Christopher, Matt	Sports	☆☆☆
FIC CLE	Cleary, Beverly	Ramona, Henry, Beezus	☆☆☆
FIC CLE	Clements, Andrew	Jake Drake	☆☆☆
FIC CON	Conford, Ellen	Jenny Archer	☆☆☆
FIC DAN	Danziger, Paula	Amber Brown	☆☆☆
FIC DEL	Delton, Judy	Pee Wee Scouts	☆☆☆

Author	Realistic Fiction Characters	Realistic Fiction Characters
Baglio, Ben	Animal Ark	☆☆☆
Blume, Judy	Fudge, Pain, Great One	☆☆☆
Cameron, Ann	Huey, Julian	☆☆☆
Child, Lauren	Clarice Bean	☆☆☆
Christopher, Matt	Sports	☆☆☆
Cleary, Beverly	Ramona, Henry, Beezus	☆☆☆
Clements, Andrew	Jake Drake	☆☆☆
Conford, Ellen	Jenny Archer	☆☆☆
Danziger, Paula	Amber Brown	☆☆☆
Delton, Judy	Pee Wee Scouts	☆☆☆

FIC BAG, FIC BLU, FIC CAM, FIC CHI, FIC CHR, FIC CLE, FIC CLE, FIC CON, FIC DAN, FIC DEL

Realistic Fiction Characters Star Review Sheet

"Students may use the following key to indicate their level of enthusiasm for each book.

☆ I probably won't check out this book.

☆ I might check out this book.

★ I definitely want to check out this book!

From *Personalized Reading: It's a Piece of PIE* by Nancy Hobbs, Kristen Sacco, and Myra R. Oleynik. Santa Barbara, CA: Libraries Unlimited. Copyright © 2011.

Call#	Author	Realistic Fiction Characters			
FIC DUF	Duffey, Betsy	Cody	☆	☆	☆
FIC GIF	Giff, Patricia Reilly	Polk Street School, Rosie	☆	☆	☆
FIC GRE	Green, Stephanie	Owen Foote	☆	☆	☆
FIC HUR	Hurwitz, Johanna	Nora, Elissa	☆	☆	☆
FIC KLI	Kline, Suzy	Horrible Harry, Herbie Jones	☆	☆	☆
FIC LOV	Lovelace, Maud Hart	Betsy and Tacy	☆	☆	☆
FIC MAR	Martin, Ann	Baby Sitter's Club / Kids in Ms. Coleman's Class	☆	☆	☆
FIC PAR	Park, Barbara	June B. Jones	☆	☆	☆
FIC PEN	Pennypacker, Sara	Clementine	☆	☆	☆
FIC RYL	Rylant, Cynthia	Cobble Street Cousins	☆	☆	☆

Call#	Author	Realistic Fiction Characters			
FIC DUF	Duffey, Betsy	Cody	☆	☆	☆
FIC GIF	Giff, Patricia Reilly	Polk Street School, Rosie	☆	☆	☆
FIC GRE	Green, Stephanie	Owen Foote	☆	☆	☆
FIC HUR	Hurwitz, Johanna	Nora, Elissa	☆	☆	☆
FIC KLI	Kline, Suzy	Horrible Harry, Herbie Jones	☆	☆	☆
FIC LOV	Lovelace, Maud Hart	Betsy and Tacy	☆	☆	☆
FIC MAR	Martin, Ann	Baby Sitter's Club / Kids in Ms. Coleman's Class	☆	☆	☆
FIC PAR	Park, Barbara	June B. Jones	☆	☆	☆
FIC PEN	Pennypacker, Sara	Clementine	☆	☆	☆
FIC RYL	Rylant, Cynthia	Cobble Street Cousins	☆	☆	☆

Realistic Fiction Characters Star Review Sheet

"Students may use the following key to indicate their level of enthusiasm for each book.

☆ I probably won't check out this book.

☆ I might check out this book.

★ I definitely want to check out this book!

Story Elements: *Dear Mrs. LaRue* by Mark Teague

Directions: *Cut out each section below. Place them in the correct order on poster paper. Label each part to create a story element summary for* Dear Mrs. LaRue.

Next, Ike felt like he was in prison at his obedience school. He was very unhappy and felt the other dogs behaved much, much worse than he did. He wrote Mrs. LaRue letters in hopes that he would get out sooner than his scheduled two months. He told Mrs. LaRue that he felt she needed him as her pet. Ike tried to get his owner to want to take him home in many different ways, like when he pretended to be sick. Finally, Ike decides he was going to escape, and he did. The towns-people and Mrs. LaRue were very worried because they didn't know where he was. After roaming for a few days, Ike returned to his city and saved Mrs. LaRue from getting hit by a truck. Mrs. LaRue was very happy to have Ike back and cooked him his favorite dinner.

Mark Teague

Ike LaRue   Mrs. LaRue

Dear Mrs. LaRue

Ike, the dog, escaped from the Igor Brotweiler Obedience School.

The story takes place at the Igor Brotweiler Canine Academy in Snort City. The story takes place in the present.

Ike, the dog, returned to Snort City and saved Mrs. LaRue from being hit by a truck.

Once my dog chewed on my favorite pair of flip-flops. I was very angry with him, just like Mrs. LaRue was when Ike ripped her coat.

First, Ike got into some trouble at home. He stole food off of the counter, howled in the night, chased cats, and tore his owner's coat. His owner, Mrs. LaRue was fed up and sent Ike to obedience school.

Fantasy

 From *Personalized Reading: It's a Piece of PIE* by Nancy Hobbs, Kristen Sacco, and Myra R. Oleynik. Santa Barbara, CA: Libraries Unlimited. Copyright © 2011.

Genre Elements Graphic Organizer

Genre:

From *Personalized Reading: It's a Piece of PIE* by Nancy Hobbs, Kristen Sacco, and Myra R. Oleynik. Santa Barbara, CA: Libraries Unlimited. Copyright © 2011.

Genre Comparison Graphic Organizer

Genre Comparison

_____ vs _____

How are the two genres alike?

How are the two genres different?

Genre:_____

Genre:_____

Picture Book Read-Alouds for Introducing Genre Elements

Realistic Fiction Picture Books

Barracca, Debra. *Adventures of Taxi Dog*

Borden, Louise. *A. Lincoln and Me*

Child, Lauren. *But, Excuse Me, That is My Book*

Fleming, Candace. *Imogene's Last Stand*

Frazee, Marla. *A Couple of Boys Have the Best Two Weeks Ever*

Harshman, Marc. *Snow Company*

Hoffman, Mary. *Amazing Grace, Boundless Grace, Princess Grace*

Juster, Norton. *Hello Goodbye Window*

Lipson, Eden Ross. *Applesauce Season*

McClosky, Robert. *Make Way for Ducklings*

O'Connor, Jane. *Fancy Nancy*

O'Neill, Alexis. *The Recess Queen*

Perkins, Lynne Rae. *Pictures from Our Summer Vacation*

Rylant, Cynthia. *The Bookshop Dog, The Cookie Store Cat*

Saltzberg, Barney, *Crazy Hair Day*

Samuels, Barbara. *Aloha Dolores, Dolores Meets Her Match*

Willems, Mo. *KnuffleBunny, KnuffleBunny Too*

Williams, Vera. *A Chair for my Mother, A Chair of my Own, A Chair for Always*

Viorst, Judith. *Alexander Who Used to be Rich Last Sunday*

Fantasy Fiction Picture Books

Agee, Jon. *Milo's Hat Trick*

Barrett, Judi. *Marshmallow Incident, Cloud with a Chance of Meatballs, Pickles to Pittsburgh*

Brett, Jan. *Trouble with Trolls*

Broach, Elise. *When Dinosaurs Came with Everything*

Carle, Eric. *Mixed Up Chameleon*

De Paola, Tomie. *Strega Nona, Strega Nona's Magic Lessons*

Fleischman, Paul. *Weslandia*

Hawkins, Colin. *Fairytale News*

Joyce, Wililam. *Dinosaur Bob*

Manushkin, Fran. *Shivers in the Fridge*

Meddaugh, Susan. *Martha Blah Blah, Cinderella's Rat*

Munsch, Robert. *Paper Bag Princess*

Nolen, Jerdine. *Balloon Farm, Raising Dragons*

O'Malley, Kevin. *Humpty Dumpty Egg-splodes*

Osborne, Mary Pope. *New York's Bravest*

Polaccco, Patricia. *Appelemando's Dreams*

Rex, Adam. *Pssst*

Schnitzlein, Danny. *The Monster Who Ate My Peas*

Seuss, Dr. *500 Hats of Bartholomew Cubbins*

Shannon, David. *Bad Case of Stripes*

Steig, William. *The Amazing Bone*

Wood, Audrey. *Heckedy Peg*

Historical Fiction Picture Books

Bartone, Elisa. *Peppe the Lamplighter*

Benchley, Nathaniel. *Sam the Minuteman*

Blake, Robert. *Akiak, Togo*

Bradby, Marie. *More Than Anything Else*

Bunting, Eve. *Dandelions*

Cooney, Barbara. *Roxaboxen*

Edwards, Pamela. *Barefoot*

Harness, Cheryl. *Three Young Pilgrims*

Hopkinson, Deborah. Sweet *Clara and the Freedom Quilt*

Houston, Gloria. *But No Candy*

Hurst, Carol Otis. *Rocks in His Head*

Kinsock-Warner. Natalie. *Bear That Heard Crying*

Levine, Ellen. *Henry's Freedom Box*

Macauley, David. *Angelo*

McKissack, Patricia. *Goin' Someplace Special*

McDonald, Megan. *The Great Pumpkin Switch*

Mochizuki, Ken. *Baseball Saved Us*

Polacco, Patricia. *The Butterfly, Pink and Say, Aunt Chip and the Triple Creek Dam Affair*

Prigger, Skillings, Mary. *Aunt Minnie McGranahan*

Ryan, Pam Munoz. *Amelia and Eleanor Go For a Ride*

Tunnell, Michael. *Mailing May*

Science Fiction

Breathed, Berkely. *Edward Fudwubber Fibbed Big*

Buehner, Carlyn. *Super Dog*

Cazet, Denys. *Minnie and Moo Save the Earth*

Clements, Andrew. *Double Trouble in Walla Walla*

Di Terlizzi, Tony. *G is for One Gzonk*

Graves, Keith. *Pet Boy*

Grey, Mini. *Traction Man is Here, Traction Man Meets Turbo Dog*

Fleischman, Paul. *Time Train*

Kirk, David. *Hush Little Alien, Nova's Ark, Moon Dogs*

Loomis, Christine. *AstroBunnies*

McLeod, Bob. *Super Hero ABC*

Peet, Bill. *The Wump World*

Pilkey, Dav. *Kat Kong, Dogzilla*

Sadler, Matthew. *Alistair in Outer Space*

Scieszka, Jon. *Henry P. Baloney*

Sierra, Judy. *The Secret Science Project that Ate the School*

Siracusa, Catherine. *The Banana Split from Outer Space*

VanAllsburg. Chris. *Zathura*

Yolen, Jane. *Commander Toad & the Space Pirates*

Mystery/Adventure Fiction Picture Books

Adler, David. *Bones and the Math Test Mystery, Bones and the Cupcake Mystery, Young Cam Jansen and the Library Mystery*

Allen, Laura Jean. *Rollo and Tweedy and the Ghost at Dougal Castle*

Cole, Bruce. *The Pumpkinville Mystery*

Cushman, Doug. *ABC Mystery, Aunt Eater Loves a Mystery, Inspector Hopper*

Devlin, Wende. *Cranberry Halloween*

Doven, Denise. *Once Upon a Twice*

Hayes, Geoffrey. *The Secret of Foghhorn Island*

Kellogg, Steven. *The Mystery Beast of Ostergeest*

Kitamura, Satoshi. *Sheep in Wolves' Clothing*

McPhail, David. *Edward and the Pirates*

Miller, Edna. *Mousekin's Mystery*

Palatini, Margie. *The Web Files*

Rylant, Cynthia. *High Rise Private Eyes series, Case of the Baffled Bear, Sleepy Sloth et. al.*

Teague, Mark. *Detective LaRue*

Tryon, Leslie. *Albert's Halloween: The Case of the Stolen Pumpkins*

Van Alsburg, Chris. *Mysteries of Harris Burdick, Bad Day at RiverBend*

Wood, Audrey. *Alphabet Mystery*

Yole, Jane. *Piggins, The Mary Celeste*

Picture Book Biographies

Adler, David. *America's Champion Swimmer, Gertrude Ederle; Lou Gehrig, The Luckiest Man*

Anholt, Laurence. *Magical Garden of Claude Monet*

Borden, Louise. *Fly High! The Story of Bessie Coleman*

Brown, Don. *One Giant Leap, The Story of Neil Armstrong*

Coles, Robert. *The Story of Ruby Bridges*

Crowe, Ellie. *Surfer of the Century: The Life Duke Kahanamoku*

Debon, Nicolas. *The Strongest Man in the World*

Gerstein, Mordicai. *The Man Who Walked Between the Towers*

Giovanni, Nikki. *Rosa*

Grimes, Nikki. *Barack Obama, Son of Hope*

Jermain, Suzanne. *George Did It!*

Kerley, Barbara. *Dinosaurs of Waterhouse Hawkins*

Krull, Kathleen. *Hillary Rodham Clinton: Dreams Taking Flight*

McCain, Meghan. *My Dad, John McCain*

Nobisso, *John Blair and the Great Hinckley Fire*

Rappaport, Doreen. *Martin's Big Words, Abe's Honest Words*

Sis, Peter. *Play Mozart Play*

Warren, Andrea. *Orphan Train Rider*

Winter, Jeannette. *Librarian of Basra*

Illustrated Poetry to Read Aloud as Background for PIE

Ashman, Linda. *The Essential Worldwide Monster Guide*

Clements, Andrew. *Dogku*

Cyrus, Kurt. *Oddhopera Opera*

Florian, Douglas. *Dinothesaurus, Summersaults, Comets, Stars, the Moon and Mars*

Foxworthy, Jeff. *Dirt on My Shirt*

Gottfried, Maya. *Good Dog!*

Howlitt, Mary Botham. *Spider and the Fly*

Janeczko, Paul. *A Poke in the I*

Johnson, Tony. *My Mexico, Mexico Mio*

Katz, Susan. *Oh Theodore! Guinea Pig Poems*

Lansky, Bruce. *Mary Had a Little Jam*

Lewis, J. Patrick. *Doodle Dandies*

Lobel, Arnold. *The Book of Pigericks, Pig Limericks*

Longfellow, Henry Wadsworth. *Paul Revere's Ride*

Maclachlan, Patricia. *Once I Ate a Pie*

Mannis, Celeste. *One Leaf Rides the Wind, Counting in a Japanese Garden*

Moore, Clement. *The Night Before Christmas*

Prelutsky, Jack. *Awful Ogre's Awful Day, Awful Ogre Running Wild*

Schertle, Alice. *Button Up! Wrinkled Rhymes*

Sidman, Joyce. *Meow Ruff*

Stevenson, James. *Cornflakes*

Worth, Valerie. *Animal Poems*

Illustrated Nonfiction as Read-Alouds or to Contrast with Fiction

Anderson, Laurie Halse. *Thank You Sarah! The Woman Who Saved Thanksgiving*

Bishop, Nic. *Frogs, Spiders, Butterflies*

Cheney, Lynne. *When Washington Crossed the Delaware*

Floca, Brian. *Moonshot*

Goldsberry, U'ilani. *A is for Aloha*

Hatkoff, Craig. *Knut: How One Little Polar Bear Captivated the World*

Jenkins, Steve. *Brothers and Sisters, Actual Size, Never Smile at a Monkey*

Leedy, Loreen. *Postcards from the Planets: Tour of the Solar System (revised edition)*

Massieloo, Ralph. *The Skull Alphabet Book*

McCarthy, Meghan. *Aliens Are Coming*

Mortenson, Greg. *Listen to the Wind: The Story of Three Cups of Tea*

Piven, Hanock. *What Presidents Are Made Of*

Rappaport, Doreen. *Lady Liberty*

Schanzer, Rosalyn. *How Ben Franklin Stole the Lightning*

Smith, Marie. *N is for Our Nation's Capital*

Suggested PIE Chapter Book Read-Alouds or Suggested Pie Book Chat Titles

Realistic Fiction

Barrows, Annie. *Ivy & Bean: Doomed to Dance*

Byars, Betsy. *Tornado*

Cleary, Beverly. *Ramona Quimby, Age 8*

Cox, Judy. *Puppy Power*

DeGroat, Diane. *Annie Pitts, Burger Kid*

Delton, Judy. Pee Wee Scouts series

Harper, Charise. *Just Grace*

Hurwitz, Johanna. *Amazing Monty*

Kelly, Katy. *Lucy Rose, Big on Plans*

Line, Grace. *Year of the Dog, Year of the Rat*

McDonald, Megan. *Stink, The Incredible Shrinking Kid*

Mills, Claudia. *Being Teddy Roosevelt*

Nagda, Ann Whitehead. *Dear Whiskers*

Park, Barbara. *Operation Dump the Chump*

Pennypacker, Sara. *Clementine: Friend of the Week*

Rockwell, Thomas. *How to Eat Fried Worms*

Fantasy Fiction

Bauer, Marion Dane. *The Very Little Princess*

Brown, Jeff. *Flat Stanley Series*

Christian, *The Bookstore Mouse*

Coville, Bruce. *The Monster's Ring*

DiCamillo, Kate. *The Magician's Elephant*

Erickson, Russell. *Toad for Tuesday*

Gannett, Ruth Stiles. *My Father's Dragon*

Hurwitz, Johanna. *Squirrel World*

LeGuin. Ursula. *Catwings*

Levine, Gail Carson. *Fairy Dust and the Quest for the Egg*

Lin, Grace, *Where the Mountain Meets the Moon*

Lubar, David. *Punished*

Martin, Ann M., *The Doll People, Meanest Doll Ever, Runaway Doll*

Osborne, Mary Pope, *Magic Treehouse series, Dinosaurs Before Dark*

Peterson, Jon. *The Littles*

Schlitz, Laura. *The Night Fairy*

Speck, Katie. *Maybelle in the Soup*

Series: Abbott, Secrets of Droon, LeGuin Catwings, Coville, Moongobble, Daisy Meadows, Rainbow Magic Fairies, Nolan, Down Girl and Sit

Historical Fiction

Ackerman, Karen. *The Night Crossing*

Bradley, Kimberly. *Ruthie's Gift*

Cohen, Barbara. *Molly's Pilgrim*

DeClements, Barth. *Bite of the Gold Bug*

Estes, Eleanor. *The Hundred Dresses*

Gutman, Dan. *Honus & Me. (time travel)*

Hill, Kirkpatrick. *The Year of Miss Agnes*

Holm, Jennifer. *Our Only May Amelia*

Myers, Laurie. *Lewis and Clark, and Me: A Dog's Tale*

Scieszka, Jon. *The Not So Jolly Roger*

Wells, Rosemary. *Lincoln and His Boys*

Science Fiction

Asch, Frank. *Star Jumper, Journal of a Cardboard Genius*

Balaban, Bob. *McGrowl, Beware of Dog*

Benton, Jim. *Franny K. Stein, Attack of the 50 Foot Cupid*

Boniface, William. *Extraordinary Adventures of Ordinary Boy*

Brown, Jeff. *Flat Stanley in Space*

Coville, Bruce. *My Teacher is an Alien*

Crilley, Mark. *Akiko on the Planet Smoo*

Etra, Jonathan. *Aliens for Breakfast*

Greenberg, Dan. *Weird Planet series: Dude, Where's My Spaceship?*

Greenberg, Dan. *Bozo the Clone*

L'Engle, Madeleine. *A Wrinkle in Time*

Palatini, Margie. *Lab Coat Girl*

Sczieska, Jon. *2095*

Mystery/Adventure Fiction

Adler, David. *Cam Jansen, Secret Service Mystery*

Dixon, Franklin. *Clues Brothers, The Walking Snowman*

Hale, Bruce. *Chet Gecko, Mystery of Mr. Nice*

Keene, Carolyn. *Nancy Drew and the Clue Crew, Sleepover Sleuths*

Levy, Elizabeth. *Invisible Inc, The Creepy Computer Mystery (also Science Fiction)*

Preller, James. *Jigsaw Jones, Case of Hermie the Missing Hamster #1*

Roy, Ron. *Capital Kids, White House White-Out*

Roy, Ron. *A-Z Mysteries Absent Author*

Sharmat, Marjorie. *Nate the Great Talks Turkey*

Simon, Seymour. *Einstein Anderson Goes to Bat*

Stilton, Geronimo. *Secret Agent*

Warner, Gertrude Chandler. *Boxcar Children*

Biography Chapter Books

Christopher, Matt. *At the Plate with Ken Griffey, Jr.*

De Paola, Tomie. *26 Fairmont Avenue*

Edgar, Geoff. *Who Was Elvis Presley?*

Edwards, Roberta. *Who Was Leonardo Da Vinci?*

Fradin, Dennis B. *Who Was Sacagawea?*

Fritz, Jean. *And Then What Happened, Paul Revere?*

Jerome, Kate Boehm. *Who Was Amelia Earhart?*

Kramer, Sydelle. *Who Was Ferdinand Magellan?*

Milton, Joyce. *Who Was Ronald Reagan?*

Pascal, Janet. B. *Who Was Abraham Lincoln?*

Stewart, Whitney. *Who Was Walt Disney?*

Weidt, Maryann N. *Oh, the Places He Went*

Poetry Collections

Ahlberg, Allan. *Everybody was a Baby Once*

Dakos, Kalli. *Put Your Eyes Up Here, If You're Not Here, Please Raise Your Hand*

DeRegniers, Beatrice Schenk. *Sing a Song of Popcorn*

Florian, Douglas. *Laugheteria, Bing! Bang! Boing!*

Hoberman, Mary Ann. *Fathers, Mothers, Sisters Brothers, Family Poems*

Lansky, Bruce. *Miles of Smiles, No More Homework! No More Tests!*

Moss, Jeff. *The Other Side of the Door*

Nesbitt, Kenn. *The Aliens Have Landed!*

Pottle, Robert. *I'm Allergic to School*

Prelutsky, Jack. *Pizza the Size of the Sun, It's Raining Pigs and Noodles*

Rex, Adam. *Frankenstein Makes a Sandwich*

Silverstein, Shel. *Runny Babbit, Where the Sidewalk Ends*

Folklore

Although folklore was not included as one of our PIE slices, it may be substituted.

Aardema, Verna. *Why Mosquitoes Buzz in People's Ears*

Boden, Alice. *The Field of Buttercups*

Deedy, Carmen Agra. *Martina the Beautiful Cockroach*

Demi. *The Empty Pot*

Ehlert, Lois. *Moon Rope*

Ernst, Lisa Campbell. *Three Spinning Fairies*

Hamilton, Virginia. *Bruh Rabbit and the Tar Baby Girl*

Knutson, Barbara. *Love and Roast Chicken*

Martin, Rafe. *Rough Face Girl*

McDermott, Gerald. *Arrow to the Sun*

Mosel, Arlene. *Tikki Tikki Tembo*

Paterson, Katherine. *The King's Equal*

Pollock, Penny. *The Turkey Girl*

Salley, Coleen. *Epossumondas*

San Souci, Robert. *Cendrillon*

Snyder, Dianne. *The Boy of the Three-Year Nap*

Stevens, Janet. *Tops & Bottoms*

Tompert, Ann. *Bamboo Hats and a Rice Cake*

Watterberg, Jane. *Henny-Penny*

Yep, Laurence. *The Boy Who Swallowed Snakes*

Zelinsky, Paul O. *Rumpelstiltskin*

Graphic Novels

Although graphic novels were not included as one of our PIE slices, it may be substituted.

Barshaw, Ruth McNally. *Ellie McDoodle, Ellie McDoodle: New Kid in School*

Burgan, Michael. *Mary Shelley's Frankenstein*

Cavallaro, Michael. *Wizard of Oz*

Davis, Terry. *H.G. Wells' The Time Machine*

Hayes, Geoffrey. *Benny and Penny in Just Pretend*

Holm, Jennifer. *Babymouse, Babymouse: Our Hero, Babymouse Burns Rubber*

Rau, Zachary. *Time Warp Trio: Nightmare on Joe's Street, Seven Blunders of the World*

Reynolds, Aaron. *Tiger Moth, Insect Ninja*

Runton, Andy. *Owly: The Way Home & the Bittersweet Summer (series)*

Scieszka, Jon; adapted by Amy Court-Kaemon. *Time Warp Trio; Meet You at Waterloo*

Telgemeier, Raina. *The Babysitter's Club; Kristy's Great Idea*

Wight, Eric. *Frankie Pickle and the Pinerun 3000*

Wood, Don. *Into the Volcano*

Nonfiction Graphic Novels as an Additional PIE Slice or as an Alternative for Reluctant Readers

DeMolay, Jack. *The Bermuda Triangle: The Disappearance of Flight 19*

Dunn, Joeming W.. *The Underground Railroad*

Gunderson, Jessica. *Young Riders of the Pony Express*

Lemke, Donald B. *The Apollo 13 Mission*

Olson, Kay M. *Benjamin Franklin: An American Genius*

Olson, Nathan. *Theodore Roosevelt: Bear of a President*

Robbins, Trina. *Besse Coleman: Daring Stunt Pilot*

Shone, Rob. *Gigantosaurus: The Giant Southern Lizard*

Sutcliffe, Jane. *The Attack on Pearl Harbor*

Appendix B

PIE-to-Go Checklist

A checklist to help teachers and librarians set up a successful PIE program for their students.

PIE-to-Go for Teachers

Before the Students Arrive

1. **Form a teacher–librarian partnership.**

   - Meet to schedule common weekly planning times.

   - Schedule Genre Overview Lesson to co-teach to class.

   - Schedule book chats throughout the year.

   - Meet to discuss possible reading lessons to support the PIE program.

2. **Prepare your room, the groups, and the materials.**

   - Create PIE folders for all students

   - Make copies of materials for each folder

     – Reading logs

     – Weekly assignment sheets

     – Books I Want to Read Sheets

     – Story element guides

     – Book sharing questions

     – Library Map

- Make copies of parent letters to be sent home with students.
- Set up meeting area and all necessary materials.
- Formulate PIE groups.

Throughout the Year

3. **Help students select books for PIE.**

   - Refer to the Top Two Ways for Teachers and Librarians to Guide the Self-Selection Process in Chapter 3.
   - Teach an introductory lesson for each genre when needed.
   - Conduct a book chat together in the library for each genre.
   - Provide assistance to students during book selection times in the library.

4. **Help students read books for PIE.**

   - Chcck reading progress of each student through weekly PIE meetings.
   - Provide time for students to read PIE books independently every day.
   - Assign PIE reading homework as nightly work.
   - Remind students to complete their reading logs as they read their books.

5. **Help students write about their books for PIE.**

   - Provide an introductory lesson for writing a story element summary (SES) for each genre when needed.
   - Direct students to complete an SES.
   - Review students' SESs for quality and accuracy.

6. **Help students share their books for PIE.**

   - Teachers and librarians meet weekly with students to share their PIE progress with their group.
   - Teachers and librarians facilitate discussion and encourage students to ask questions of each other in PIE groups.
       Direct students to write the title of the book and color in that genre slice of their PIE after sharing their SES with the group

7. **Help students extend their books for PIE.**

   - Direct students to choose one of the books from their PIE and create an extension project.
   - Allow students to share their extension projects with their PIE groups and possibly other members of the school or community.
   - After completion of the extension project, direct students to begin another PIE chart and start the process again.

PIE-to-Go for Librarians

Before The Students Arrive:

1. **Form a teacher–librarian partnership.**

   - Start with one teacher.

   - Schedule a common weekly planning time and meet regularly.

   - Schedule Genre Overview Lessons to co-teach to class.

   - Plan ahead and schedule future book chats throughout the year.

   - Collaborate to connect language arts curriculum objectives that also relate to PIE into lessons taught through the library.

2. **Prepare the library.**

   - Inventory your collection for gaps in genres, number of copies, and condition.

   - Check your circulation statistics for the most popular PIE checkouts and order more copies accordingly.

   - Be sure that all books are labeled with genre spine labels and are in good condition.

   - Reinforce spines of paperbacks to extend the lives of the books.

   - Display several PIE projects from previous years to spark interest.

   - Create links for student access to your library wiki, blog, or website to extend PIE at home.

   - Keep up with reading reviews and new titles.

   - Seek out "sleepers" on the shelves to add to book chats and displays.

Throughout the Year

   - Support the teacher's PIE-to-Go Checklist.

   - Meet and greet PIE books with students on a daily basis.

   - Seek out students who need extra help with self-selection.

   - Reconnect with students in the halls and ask them, "What are you reading for PIE?" "Are you almost ready for a new PIE book?" "Oh Jake, I set aside a great new book that I thought you might like to consider for PIE."

   - Browse through PIE genre displays to remove random books that don't belong.

   - Rotate unselected books out to freshen up the various genre displays with different choices.

   - Schedule book chats and update star review forms as needed.

   - Add new buttons and search strategies to your library's OPAC.

- Post banners, signs, and familiar symbols to direct students to PIE displays. Note the acronym Personalized, Independent Enrichment.

- Keep plenty of CAT slips and sharp pencils handy.

- Take "Get Caught Reading" pictures of students to post throughout the library or school reading their favorite books.

- Update showcases and bulletin boards to highlight new choices for PIE.

- Keep reading.

- Continue to reinforce book spines.

- Survey students to gain insight into popular favorites.

- Add a suggestion box for more titles.

- Encourage volunteers or library staff to put books on hold for students who are waiting for PIE books.

- Schedule formal lessons on the use of the OPAC, filling out CAT slips and using guide words to help students become more confident in locating PIE books.

- Plan technology lessons for students and staff.

- Sprinkle technology throughout lessons to build confidence among students and staff as well as confidence in your own abilities.

- Review PIE procedures with parent volunteers or library staff.

- Schedule a formal training with library volunteers so they can help students be successful with PIE.

- Invite the principal to drop in to see students involved in self-selection for PIE and encourage the principal to talk to students about their book choices.

- Update slideshows with new pictures for digital picture frames to display through the library.

- Interview students for weekly school news broadcasts.

- Create new scavenger hunts for PIE genres throughout the library.

- Add screensavers to library computer desktops featuring students with favorite PIE books.

- Keep reading.

- Use lots of positive praise.

- Be flexible.

Index

Note: Page numbers followed by an f indicate figures; page numbers followed by a t indicate tables.

About the Authors

NANCY HOBBS currently teaches third grade in the Peters Township School District, McMurray, PA. Nancy has taught grades K through 6 and served as an elementary school administrator for four years in both Indiana and Pennsylvania. Nancy earned her doctorate degree from the University of Pittsburgh in Administrative and Policy Studies.

KRISTEN SACCO currently teaches third grade in the Peters Township School District, McMurray, PA. Kristen has been a teacher for 17 years in both Pennsylvania and Nevada. Additionally, she has served as an elementary guidance counselor in the Las Vegas area. Kristen earned her bachelor's degree from Indiana University of Pennsylvania and a master's degree in elementary school counseling from the University of Nevada Las Vegas.

MYRA R. OLEYNIK has been a K to 5 library media specialist in the Peters Township School District, McMurray, PA, for the past 14 years. She began her career in education as a classroom teacher where she taught first, second, third, and fifth grades. She received her MLS degree from the University of Pittsburgh and currently serves as a K to 3 library media specialist for 800 students at Bower Hill Elementary, Venetia, PA, recently named Outstanding Library Media Center in Pennsylvania. Myra is also a Keystone Technology Integrator and Pennsylvania Teacher Excellence Honoree.